THE LOVE-EXPLOSION

THE LOVE-
EXPLOSION

Human Experience
and the Christian Mystery

Robert E. Lauder

Grateful acknowledgement is made to *The Long Island Catholic* for some material which previously appeared in its pages.

Nihil Obstat: Martin S. Rushford, Diocesan Censor.

Imprimatur: Francis J. Mugavero, D.D., Bishop of Brooklyn, Brooklyn, New York, December 28, 1978.

Cover: Robert Manning

Published by: Living Flame Press/Locust Valley/New York 11560.

Printed in the United States of America.

248.4

*To Ellin and Frank
with gratitude for their loving presence.*

Contents

Introduction

Persons are made for love. Though this insight is easy to articulate, so easy that it can be found under various forms in popular songs, contemporary theatre, film, literature and poetry, on banners, tee shirts and car bumpers, a serious understanding of its meaning raises important questions about the meaning of human existence. While many can correctly extol love's values, few wish to think through its demands and even fewer wish to live up to those demands.

In Dostoyevsky's masterpiece, *The Brothers Karamazov*, Father Zossima says "Love is a terrible thing." The same sentiment was echoed by E.E. Cummings: "Be of love a little more careful than of anything." While the popular song's refrain "Love makes the world go round" is accurate, love can also cause revolution, war, tragedy and heartbreak. All the paradoxes of love are eminently evident in a young Jewish religious leader's death on a cross. That he freely consented to it reveals that love does such things. Because Americans are an active people, and in the last quarter of the twentieth century vacillate between hyperactivity and exhaustion, because the worlds of business and leisure seem more action-oriented than ever, reflections on the mystery of love can seem abstract, speculative and even unreal. Many think such reflections should be reserved for the poets and philosophers who don't seem to live in the real world with the rest of hustling, bustling humanity. Yet this book is written in the belief that the real world is a turf that will become more real through love and less real through lack of love, that rather than being abstract love is the most concrete activity, an incarnation of the self, and the reflections on love are most practical if the human endeavor is to make ultimate sense, or indeed any sense at all.

When a deep love experience enters a person's life a sense of wonder usually accompanies it: the person never realized that life could be this way, that being human included something like this. Though there may be some truth to the dictum "Love is blind" the experience of love often opens eyes, sometimes in a startling and powerful way. For this and other reasons, especially its power to redirect the lives of both lovers and those who are loved, I call this book the "love-explosion." The explosion may take various forms: parental love, conjugal love, heterosexual and homosexual love, the love of a religious minister for his community, of a teacher for his students, of a friend for a friend. Whatever its form, if it is love something uniquely powerful, immensely exciting and a little frightening has appeared in human relationships.

The love-explosion took place in a special way on the first Easter. Those who profess the Christian religion, which in its earliest days and at various times in its history has caused people to remark, "See how these Christians love one another," look to Easter and the risen Lord for the most profound meaning of love. St. Paul, overwhelmed by love, claimed that he accepted the loss of everything and looked on everything as so much rubbish if only he could have Christ (*Philippians 3:8*) and Christians in their encounter with the Risen Christ have made similar judgments. The great task today, and perhaps it has always been humanity's task, is to make sense of experience, to find and form some meaningful pattern from the apparently random events that clutter a life, to eventually "put it all together." For the Christian, essential to putting it all together is seeing the relationship between personal experience and the presence of the Risen Lord. The "human experience" in the title of this book is not restricted to any one type of experience such as sense experience or bodily experience or intellectual experience, but is to be understood in the broadest possible sense. By human experience is meant personal presence to others, including personal presence to Other. By the Christian mystery is meant the Paschal Event — the Birth, Death, Resurrection and Ascension of Christ, including the presence of the Risen Lord today to the human community. Christians must see the risen life is love life and must incarnate and incorporate that love life into daily experience. The explosion that happened on Easter must happen again and again so that there might be new Easters throughout the human community.

There is just nothing that can equal love's role in human development. It is both the source and the secret of human life and happiness. Persons are made for love.

1

The Mystery of Love

People don't like mysteries. Or at least they don't like mysteries that are not solvable. Murder mysteries are interesting reading because we know that at the end of the book the villain will be caught. The human mind has a natural drive to know and understand and when that drive runs up against a brick wall, frustration is experienced. I remember vividly my feelings when reading a paperback novel on vacation recently. I discovered as I reached what I thought was the end of the book that the last few pages had fallen out and were lost. Somehow the time spent reading nine tenths of the book seemed wasted. Without that missing one tenth, the other nine tenths didn't add up to a book. Whatever meaning the book seemed to have fell apart without the ending.

Love is not a mystery in the same sense that a novel in which the murderer is not revealed until the last pages is a mystery. Nor is it a mystery in the sense of a science or math problem to which we don't yet know the answer. Love is a special kind of mystery. Unlike whodunits or science and mathematics problems, love had no final solution or answer. This is because love is more, not less, rich than whodunits and science and math problems. There is a richness in love, a depth in love, a wealth of value in love that exceeds our capacity to completely understand. The brightest student of whodunits and the finest scientists and mathematicians could never completely understand the mystery of loving.

The special type of mystery about which we are talking was described very well by Frank Sheed in his utterly delightful *Theology and Sanity*. Though Sheed was talking specifically about mysteries of religion, what he said applies to the mystery of love. Pointing out that the mind can never totally comprehend all of reality, Sheed wrote:

> *At first thought this might seem a reason for abandoning the whole venture: if Reality is so utterly beyond us, why not leave it alone and make the best terms we can with our ineluctable darkness? But a Mystery is not something that we can know nothing about: it is only something that the mind cannot **wholly** know. It is not to be thought of as a high wall that we can neither see over nor get around: it is to to be thought of rather as a gallery into which we can progress deeper and deeper, though we can never reach the end — yet every step of our progress is immeasurably satisfying. A Mystery in short is an*

*invitation to the mind. For it means that
there is an inexhaustible well of Truth
from which the mind may drink and drink
again in the certainty that the well will
never run dry, that there will always be
water for the mind's thirst.*[1]

Catholic existentialist Gabriel Marcel made a
distinction between problem and mystery.[2] A
problem is something external to us, something that
does not involve our personal life, and to which
there is a solution. Even though we might not know
what the solution is, a problem in principle always
has a solution. Whodunits and scientific and
mathematical problems are not mysteries in
Marcel's sense of the term but merely problems. The
expression "merely problems" is consonant with
Marcel's vision because for the French thinker
mysteries were infinitely more important than
problems. A mystery involved an individual
personally. It was so deep that its meaning could
never be exhausted. For this reason there was no
solution. A person can uncover much of its meaning
but a mystery is an inexhaustible source of truth and
a spur to wonder. Love is a mystery in this sense.

That it is more important to love than to have
insights into love doesn't mean that reflection on
love and on love experiences is pointless. To reflect
on the meaning and mystery of love is to involve
yourself in important questions about the meaning
of human existence, of religion and, indeed, about
the meaning of all of reality.

To be human is to be involved in multiple relationships and in multiple desires and dreams. Besides all the nonpersonal objects in our life, we relate to parents, brothers and sisters, children, other relatives, friends, neighbors, co-workers, acquaintances and God. Our desires seem unlimited in number — food and drink, work, a home, knowledge, a family, prestige, power and so forth. Our desires are so many that any list would hardly even suggest their number or variety but they all center around our personal fulfillment. To be human seems to be to stretch toward some kind of utopian existence in which we will exist in a way that we have never existed previously, a heavenly existence in which the cup of our being will run over, a life in which pain and lack are replaced by pleasure and fullness. Whatever this desire to exist in a new way might mean, any attempt to understand it will have to focus on the meaning of love.

A sketch of the love dynamic between two people will provide a background against which the remaining chapters can be read. In this discussion the two people need not be married or of the opposite sex. What we are after are certain key aspects or moments of every love relationship, whether it be between man and woman, man and man, or man and God. We want to reflect on the meaning of the mystery of loving whenever and wherever it is found. For the purpose of clarity we will call the two members of the relationship the lover and the beloved. Though the ideal relationship is one in which the lover is loved by the person whom he loves, we will confine ourselves to a discussion of the lover purely as lover and not as one who is loved in return. Accordingly, we will talk about the beloved as one who *is* loved and not as one who loves.[3]

For the love relationship to begin the lover must notice something extremely important about the beloved, namely that the beloved *is* a call to the lover. While some attractive feature or physical characteristic may attract the attention of the lover, there is a more important and radical sense in which the beloved is a call to the lover. To catch this sense we must go beyond all physical characteristics and bodily features to who the beloved is. The beloved on the deepest level of the self is a center, a core, a uniqueness that is absolutely unrepeatable. The beloved as a peson is a free, mysterious subject who has physical characteristics and bodily features and other qualities. What is being said about the beloved is true of every person: the most physically attractive person and the ugliest person, the most intelligent and most stupid, the clever, the witty and the dull. To be a person is to be someone important, a magnificent mystery, whether one's appearance makes that easy to observe or seems to conceal it.

Years ago Father Faber, the noted spiritual author, suggested that the most basic act of faith that a person must make is in his own uniqueness as a gift from God's creative hand. Out of billions and billions of possible individuals, God created me. If I really believe that God chose to create me, not just as part of a group, not just as one of many, but as a unique, unrepeatable individual, then I can have a true sense of my importance. I didn't just happen — God decided to create the unique, individual person I am, this particular special imitation of himself, God created me as a treasure of possibilities, as an openness who can face the future with trust and courage because of God's creative choice.

Every person is a treasure who needs others. On the deepest level of the self every person is a call and a need for other persons. To be a person is to need the help of others. To be a person is to be someone who can grow only through relationships with others. To have this need is not something that a person has any choice about: it is true of every person whether an individual wishes to admit it or not. It is part and parcel of what being a person means.

For love to happen the lover must first notice that the beloved is this need or call. If the lover does not notice this, if the lover does not "hear" the call that the beloved personifies then love cannot happen. Another way of saying this is that if the lover does not eventually focus on the "you" then love cannot happen because love always focuses on the you. While expressions such as "I love your hair" or "I love your eyes" are common, they are not accurate expressions. It would be more proper to say "I really like your hair" or "I find your eyes very attractive." Love always focuses on the you. Love is always a self-gift and no one is going to give himself to someone else's hair or eyes. I only give myself to a you.

On first reflection it may seem easy for a lover to notice the need or call that a beloved represents, to notice the beloved as a you who needs the help of other persons. Experience reveals that it is not easy. The reasons are numerous. First there is the tendency toward selfishness in all of us. I am so preoccupied with myself, so interested in myself that I can easily fall into that habit of bypassing people, of not noticing people, of reducing people to their functions and roles in society. It's not that I deliberately decide to do this but rather that my self-centeredness clouds my consciousness, blurs my conscience and dulls my sensitivity.

Another reason is that the society in which I live encourages me to reduce people to their roles or jobs. This person can't be very important because he is only a maintenance man in a school; that person must be important because he is a successful lawyer. We are encouraged to make value judgments about people by the clothes they wear, the places in which they live, the salaries they make. How can I spot the uniqueness of anyone when I keep putting people in slots or boxes according to some function they perform? Someone has described our society as the "disposable society" — as long as you can perform a useful function you have some worth; when you can't perform you are shipped off to an institution.

That it is not necessary to reduce people to their functions or roles, that it is really inhuman to do so, was brought home to me vividly and rather touchingly, at the wake of my sister. A victim of leukemia, my sister died at the age of thirty-six, leaving two small children. At the wake countless people came to comfort the family and to say how much she meant in their lives. Many found my sister's courage and faith in facing death extremely inspiring. Though I tried to stand strongly during the wake and not be overcome by my emotions, twice there were moments when I almost lost control. In the crowded funeral parlor I suddenly noticed two men approaching me whom I recognized immediately but whose presence at the wake stunned me. They were two santitation men who picked up the garbage in the neighborhood where my family lived. When I mentioned that I was surprised to see them one of the men explained to me how pleasant and friendly my sister always was to them. He indicated that my sister treated them differently, that she was someone special. Later some cafeteria workers from the school where my sister had a prestigious job before marriage came to me and said how special she was to them, and how her kind friendly disposition had meant so much to them. To those who reduce people to their roles or functions, sanitation men and cafeteria workers might seem to be unimportant people but my sister made a difference in their lives and on the occasion of her death they made a difference in mine.

Another reason why the lover may not spot the unique need or call that the beloved embodies is that our society puts such an enormous price tag on physical qualities. Your figure makes you lovable, your face makes you lovable, your smell makes you lovable! Love is often reduced to an attraction to some physical characteristic. If that physical characteristic is missing then the person is not lovable. This attitude toward people, and numerous other factors, can easily distract the lover from noticing the unique call that the beloved is. Every person is uniquely beautiful regardless of their physical characteristics. What made the 1977 award winning film *Rocky* so popular with large audiences was that it was a love story about two "losers" who find out that lovers are never losers.

If the lover does recognize the call that the beloved represents then a response is required. Life cannot proceed as usual for the lover: the lover must say yes or no to the call or try to avoid it which is in effect a negative response. Rightly, the lover feels threatened by the presence of the beloved. The reason for this is that the call occurs on the most radical level of the person's being, and it is on this level that the response must be made. The beloved *is* the call. The call and appeal on the part of the beloved is not for something that the lover possesses. If the lover could satisfy the request of the beloved with some possession the lover would not be so threatened. The request of the beloved is "Accompany me, be with me, support me, help me to be a person." No possession that the lover has can be substituted for the lover himself.

If, when the lover perceives the call and realizes what is being asked of him, he freely answers yes, then he has chosen to love. Of course we don't mean the word yes but rather the lover's gift of self. Love is being for the other, being in favor of the other, being

21

available for the other, being at the service of the other. With his gift of self the lover in effect says to the beloved, "I am for you. My person is present as a gift for the benefit of your person." Though through the ages lovers have thought of much more romantic expressions than my "person is present as a gift for the benefit of your person," no matter how they express the reality, love always means a self-gift. This is why the experience of loving is so marvelous and mysterious: it takes place at the deepest level of the person's being. It is also why we are afraid to love — because we know it will cost us ourselves. C.S. Lewis expressed this well.

> To love at all is to be vulnerable. Love anything, and your heart will certainly be wrung and possibly broken. If you want to make sure of keeping intact, you must give your heart to no one, not even to an animal. Wrap it carefully round with hobbies and little luxuries, avoid entanglements, lock it up safe in the casket or coffin of your selfishness. But in that casket — safe, dark, motionless, airless — it will change. It will not be broken; it will become unbreakable, impenetrable, irredeemable. The alternative to tragedy, or at least to the risk of tragedy, is damnation. The only place outside Heaven where you can be perfectly safe from all the dangers and perturbations of love is Hell.[4]

Because love is so powerful and because it is

often accompanied by strong emotions and passions, it can be mistakenly identified as a feeling. Though often accompanied by the most powerful feelings, love is not a feeling. Love is a free choice. A person loves whom a person chooses to love. A man may feel a very strong attraction to a beautiful woman. He does not love her until he makes himself present as a gift to her. Love must take place face to face, person to person. The women's liberation movement is calling attention to the nature of love indirectly when it proclaims that women no longer want to be sex objects. What is implied is that men reduce women to their physical qualities and relate to an "it" rather than a "thou." That kind of relating is not love. Though many men must have found Marilyn Monroe extremely attractive it would be difficult to call their way of relating to her through her films and photographs love. In fact the very image that was promoted through her publicity blurred any image of a real person. As a sex goddess Miss Monroe's real personality was concealed. Some of the accounts of her life, written after her death, suggest that she eventually took her life because she didn't feel that anyone was interested in her as a unique person rather than as a glamour girl, movie star or sex object. It is sadly paradoxical that it is easier to know the real Marilyn Monroe after her death than during her life. The absurdity of her death may be an illustration of the truth that the absence of love makes life absurd.

Feelings can be aroused by all sorts of things. Love can only be freely chosen. What is most physically attractive a person might not choose to love; what is physically repellant a person might choose to love. I imagine that if Mother Teresa of Calcutta allowed her feelings to rule her life she never would have pursued her apostolate to the lepers. Each of us can think of examples from his own life. I can vividly recall visiting a dying friend of mine in the hospital. This person's friendship had a profound effect on my life. We had been friends for ten years and his friendship had profoundly influenced me. He was dying but had not yet been anointed. When I entered the hall of the hospital I met the chaplain who asked if I would like to anoint my friend. As I anointed him, the cancer that racked his body made him seem like another person. He could hardly speak. He could barely breathe. All my feelings told me to run from the room. I didn't feel like being there; I didn't feel like facing my friend's death with him. But I stayed and anointed him and a day later when he died, I knew that I had been greatly blessed. My love for him had been blessed: I was privileged to serve him at the end.

So loving is a free choice. Paradoxically, it is through a surrender and a gift of self that the self grows in a way that has few parallels. The paradox of personal existence is that through dying we live, through giving we receive, through surrendering we conquer. The lover discovers a dimension of his existence of which he was unaware before he loved. He finds out that he is never more a person than when he is loving. He discovers that he is never better than when he is giving himself away. The lover discovers that it is very important for him that he be able to love. If there is no one who will receive his love, then he can't develop as a person because personal growth takes place not merely through being loved but through loving. It is not just that persons have a profound need to be loved, they have a profound need to love.

It is precisely this need of love and the inability to make contact with a beloved that is one of the key elements in much contemporary drama and film. The theater of the absurd, from Beckett's *Krapp's Last Tape* to Pinter's *The Birthday Party*, dramatizes the tremendous need that persons have to communicate but on the stage of the absurd no meaningful contact can be made. Persons keep calling but there is no one on the other end of the phone.

More than any other contemporary filmmaker the Swedish genius Ingmar Bergman has brilliantly characterized contemporary man's search for love. Since *The Seventh Seal* in 1957 and *Face to Face* in 1976, Bergman has vacillated from minimal hopefulness to the brink of despair. In a particularly powerful film, the title for which Bergman takes from St. Paul's hymn to love in Chapter 13 of I Corinthians, he explores the relationships between a father, his daughter, son, son-in-law and God. Though various interpretations of *Through a Glass Darkly* have been offered, there is no doubt that the film ends on a hopeful note. Though the daughter is taken away to an insane asylum, her suffering has provided the opportunity for the father, who has been cold and distant, to relate to his seventeen year-old son, who has been searching for an identity. The girl's sickness enables the father to open up and to communicate with his son. The following is the dialogue between the son, Minus, and his father, David, at the end of the film after the son has asked for some sign of God, some sign of hope in an apparently meaningless world:

David: It's written: God is love.

Minus: For me that's just words and nonsense.

David: Wait a moment and don't interrupt. I only want to give you an indication of where my own hopes lie.

Minus: Of course it's a special sort of love you're referring to.

David: *Every* sort of love, Minus! The the highest and the lowest, and the poorest and the richest, the most ridiculous and the most sublime. The obsessive and the banal. All sorts of love.

Minus: (Silent) Longing for love.

David: Longing and denial. Disbelieving and being consoled.

Minus: So love is the proof?

David: We can't know whether love proves God's existence or

whether love is itself God. After all, it doesn't make very much difference.

Minus: For you God and love are one and the same phenomenon.

David: If I let my emptiness, my dirty hopelessness, rest in that thought, yes.

Minus: Tell me, Daddy.

David: Suddenly the emptiness turns into wealth, and hopelessness into life. It's like a pardon, Minus. From sentence of death.[5]

After the dialogue between them ends, the father enters the house to cook dinner. Facing the camera Minus says, "Daddy spoke to me!" In the very dialogue of love, love has been experienced!

While it is true that loving fulfills the lover, it is also true that the experience of being loved can transform the beloved. The loving presence of the lover provides for the beloved a reality that cannot be provided by the beloved himself or by any reality less than a person. No object or thing, no matter how powerful, can match the power that loving has to influence and change the one loved. The power that the lover has can best be described as creative. A person can make all sorts of things such as chairs, tables, automobiles and other useful artifacts but persons cannot create something from nothing. Only God can do that. We talk about artists creating masterpieces but even with the greatest masterpiece the artist, for all his genius, did not really create a reality from nothing. This is not possible for human beings. The closest that a person can come to creating is through loving. Though a lover does not create the way God creates, in loving the lover imitates God in his act of creation. The lover can bring about a new person in the beloved. The lover can "create" the beloved into a new you. No activity except loving can do this. Of course if the beloved does not receive the love offered, if the beloved closes himself to the love offered by the lover then nothing happens. But if the beloved opens himself to the love offered by the lover then the beloved can grow as a person. Lovers go about "creating" those they love. They fill, they support, they release, they free. Parents do this for children, wives for husbands, teachers for students, priests for people, friends for those they love.

Numerous examples could be provided. The presence of the lover is so liberating that he is a constant freeing and creative presence. Because of this constancy, specific moments of special creativity can be missed. I know that when I have a difficult decision to make, when I have to take a risk that frightens me, the loving support of friends makes the decision easier to make and the risk less frightening. Just a couple of words from those who love us can act like mountains of energy in relation to freedom. Recently I had to give an important retreat to prospective deacons. Because I had never done this before and because I knew that the seminarians were expecting something special, I became quite apprehensive about it. I mentioned this to a friend of mine, a wife and mother whose own obligations and duties fill a twenty-four-hour day. Days after I mentioned this to her, I visited her and her husband (on the eve of the retreat) on my way to the retreat house. I could tell that she was concerned about my apprehension. As I left she called out, "Don't worry. You'll be great." Just a few simple words, but coming out of the context of our relationship they meant a great deal to me. Words from our friends, words from those who care about us carry a special message.

After the retreat I was going on a vacation. Two friends of mine went out of their way to contact me and tell me they would miss me. They meant it. They really would miss me! What can seem small and insignificant takes on a new importance when it comes from those who love us.

The presence of a lover can be represented in a few words or in a handshake or a touch or an embrace. What it always means is "I am for you." Lovers are always telling those they love that they matter, that they count, that they are significant. The meaning "I love you" may be enunciated in a phone call or in a marriage relationship; it may take seconds to communicate or it may take a lifetime. Whatever the form or the time, love is a freeing creative power. From the moment we are born, and in a special way after we can act freely, the loving presence of others creates us.

In this general discussion of the experience of

loving and being loved we have touched on four
different aspects of love, four different moments of
love: call, free response, fulfillment of the lover and
creative freeing of the beloved. These four moments
are important and can be found in some way in all
successful love relationships. Human experience
can seem to be a disordered, even chaotic affair. It
isn't. If life is a blind date, love is the clue to its
success.

Discussion Questions on Introduction and Chapter 1

1. Do people think discussions of love are
   abstract? Why?

2. Why is love a "terrible thing"? Why should we
   be "of love a little more careful than of
   anything"?

3. What is meant by human experience in the
   title? What is meant by the Christian Mystery
   in the title?

4. In what sense is love a mystery? What is
   attractive about the kind of mystery that love
   is?

5. Why must we appeal to the meaning and
   mystery of love in order to make sense of our
   desires?

6. What does it mean to say the beloved is a call
   and an appeal?

7. What in our society distracts a potential lover from noticing that the beloved is a call or an appeal?

8. What is the love response? Is it a feeling?

9. What does it mean to say love is creative?

10. What are the four moments of love?

2

Love and Personal Existence

The Christian religion has fallen on tough times. At least there is a great deal of evidence which seems to suggest this. Though there are some signs that indicate a religious revival it is difficult to tell how authentic, deep or widespread the revival is or might become. However, it is possible to see some of the reasons why the Christian religion is in crisis today. The contemporary view of man and world which many people, either consciously or without much deliberation, have accepted militates against the Christian interpretation of experience.

In his excellent *Naming the Whirlwind: The Renewal of God Language* (The Bobbs-Merrill Company, New York, 1969) Langdon Gilkey explores and explains in detail the problems that religion, and more specifically the Christian religion has today. Gilkey's book is a brilliant analysis and one that offers many insights into contemporary man's self-understanding. In the book Gilkey discusses four characteristics of what he calls the secular spirit, that spirit which colors man's experience, his self-understanding and his

32

understanding of reality.[1] I will use the four characteristics to illustrate that the vision of life which many have settled for is, if not hostile, at least antithetical to religion. The four characteristics are contingency, relativity, temporality and autonomy. Though the four words have a technical ring to them, what they mean in terms of human experience is fairly easy to grasp. The basic point is that these four characteristics make it difficult for people to think about God in traditional terms. The following is a sketch of a vision of reality using the four characteristics, a vision accepted by many today.

The sense of contingency seems to color all of contemporary man's experience. Possibly the best example to illustrate the contemporary experience of contingency is evolution. The existence of man is totally due to the evolutionary process. That process could have taken a number of different directions but it didn't. It happened to go one way out of an infinitely possible number of ways. No divine intelligence fashioned man and there is no goal for man beyond this world, no final home offered by a personal God. In other words, there is no intelligent purpose built into evolution. The process of evolution is totally physical or material and the direction that evolution has taken is largely due to chance. Thus while contemporary man admits that there are causes and effects, he no longer believes that there is a First Cause who is intelligent and who is providentially guiding man's life. Contemporary man sees dependency and contingency throughout his experience. Unlike St. Thomas, contemporary man does not conclude that there must be a God upon whom all this dependency rests. Contemporary man settles for the experience of dependency. Today, with the secular spirit or mood coloring man's consciousness, the experience of contingency does not lead beyond this world.

The second characteristic, relativity, suggests that there are no absolute truths. Today man has a sense that nothing is unalterable, nothing escapes the process of change. Everything is relative: the human species, political and social structures, the noblest of ideas, the highest aspirations, the most sacred scriptures and holy books, all institutions, including the Church. All things are conditioned by their environment. There are no absolute moral truths and no divine revelation that has application to all places and to all times. Everything is in flux, everything is in the process of change. Both practices and theories seem to have the stability and solidity of mercury.

The third characteristic is temporality or transience. Both exciting and challenging, the temporal order is not only meaningful to contemporary man but his experience of it is so strong that it cancels out the eternal as meaningless. All things have a beginning and an end. Transience pervades man's experience. The only meaning that man seems to have is meaning limited to his temporal experience. Contemporary man has a new sense of historicity. The vision of contemporary man is time bound in a way that is radically new.

Gilkey expresses succinctly but well the pervasiveness of transience and the temporal in man's experience:

All is becoming, all is changing, all is in passage out of the past and into the future, and so all causes and all effects come and go — and all is mortal — and nothing else is real.[2]

Sometimes the experience of time leads to pessimism, sometimes to optimism. The important point is that contemporary man has difficulty conceiving of anything or anyone non-temporal or eternal.

The fourth characteristic, autonomy, is related to contemporary man's sense of responsibility. He feels in charge of his life, in control of existence. The first three characteristics put religion in a difficult position: they put pressures on traditional theism and the Christian view of man, at least as it has been traditionally formulated. The fourth characteristic can offer some hope — in fact, it may be the tool to lead us into a deeper and more fruitful Christian faith.

If a person's vision of life is totally structured by the first three characteristics, then it is difficult to see how Christianity will succeed in speaking to him. There doesn't seem to be any room for Christian truth in a vision of life that only allows for contingency, relativity and temporality. Autonomy, man's freedom, his capacity to be self-creative is the power by which he can shatter horizons and break into new worlds. The Christian religion can seem to have fallen on tough times, but perhaps man's freedom, encouraged by God's love, will lead to a second spring. The meaning of personal existence can tell us about the meaning of freedom, and the meaning of freedom can tell us about the meaning of love. The meaning of freedom and love has to be understood within a mosaic made up of important aspects of personal existence. That the jewels of freedom and love may shine more brightly and that their light might lead us more deeply into the Christian mystery, we will focus attention on the meaning of personal existence.

Different aspects of personal existence highlight the meaning of both freedom and love. We will use four key characteristics of personal existence — relation, presence, transcendence and response — to probe more deeply into the mystery of freedom and love.

A person is a being who is relational. Though that may seem an awkward expression, it says something profound about personhood. In traditional thought what was emphasized was a substance of a person. Stress was put upon the truth that a person was a being distinct from other beings and was the center of conscious and free activity. Of course much more was said about personhood in traditional thought, but what was not emphasized was that a person in his very being is openness to other beings. The key point is not that a person *can* open himself to others but that the very *being* of a person involves openness. A person can decide how he will relate but not that he will relate. This is the significance of saying that a person is relational. Built into personal existence is a need for the other.

The most obvious evidence that a person is relational is on the level of knowing, or consciousness and willing. A person doesn't ever merely know. He always knows *something*. A person is never merely conscious. He is always conscious of something. There is no such reality as consciousness. What I mean is that consciousness is always "consciousness of." The same point can be made about willing and choosing. A person does not just will or choose. He wills or chooses something. In other words, consciousness and willing demand objects, they demand another. A person who is conscious and willing is on the deepest level of his being relational.

In recent years the words "relationship" and "relating" have assumed a new importance in the vocabulary of many. To ask "How are you relating to your situation?" or "How are you relating to your spouse?" is almost to ask "How are you?" Relating is so important, so essential to a person's being that relating can become a truly existential problem. How you relate indicates how you are. Indeed it indicates who you are. Contemporary thought has illuminated for us the importance of how and to what a person relates. One important instance of the importance of relation is not in the statement "You are what you eat" but in the statement "You are what you love."

I can understand my whole life in terms of my relationships. I relate to the seminary building where I teach in one way, I hope I relate to the college seminarians in another way. Though I try to relate in an open and caring way to many, I know that there are a handful of people in my life to whom I relate in a special way. These are my closest friends, those whom I love most deeply. If my relationship with any of these people is disturbed in any way I am bothered and upset. My existential equilibrium is tilted and my life seems out of kilter. I have to improve the relationship or smoothe out the difficulty. Until I do, my loving and work are seriously hampered.

Perhaps I am hypersensitive but I feel very deeply about my friendships and am easily hurt by any lack of interest, concern or love shown me by those I hold dear. Though I make acquaintances easily and can quickly establish a pleasant and easy-going relationship, I don't easily open my deepest self to people and when I do I expect, rightly or wrongly, a care and concern on the part of the other. Reflecting on my way of relating reveals to me my best and worst self. When I do give I give myself deeply but perhaps I should be less hesitant to give.

The notion of presence is closely connected to the notion of relation but is not identical to it. The notion of presence is connected to *how* a person is open to others and relates to others. Objects can be present but persons are present in a way that is unique to them. Even within personal presence various types and various intensities of presence are possible.

The most obvious and minimal kind of personal presence is mere physical presence. Imagine that you are attending a class. Neither the subject matter nor the teacher of the class interests you. It's a hot summer afternoon and your mind wanders toward a beach. You'd prefer to be there, taking an occasional swim and enjoying the warm rays of sun rather than to be enduring the discomfort of the classroom. You fantasize so much about the beach that you have no knowledge at all of what is going on in the classroom. While we would have to say that you are present in the classroom, your presence is minimal. You're there but you're almost not there. It's a different situation if you are intensely interested in both the subject and the teacher's insights and observations about the subject. Then you would be more personally present, more intensely present.

The situation is different if you are with your best friend, sharing a profoundly moving experience. Here you are present in a very special way. It's analogous to being present in prayer to God. Somehow presence to a friend or presence in loving prayer to God is personal presence in the most special, exalted sense. We sense that in these last two instances we achieve our personhood, we are persons in a way that we are not in our other activities. We sense that these activities make incarnate the deepest meaning of personal existence.

There is a marvelous anecdote illustrating the

value of presence in Martin Buber's *Between Man and Man*.[3] In relating the anecdote, Buber confessed how in his early years he thought of the "religious" as the exceptional, as the special, as that which was extraordinary. For him religious experience was an experience of otherness which did not fit into everyday life. Somehow the "religious" lifted you out of the everyday. The wrongness of such a view came home to him after an experience he had with a young man. Buber relates that after a morning of religious enthusiasm (perhaps it was a morning of prayer), he was visited by an unknown young man. Though he was friendly with the young man and conversed pleasantly with him, Buber did not guess the question which the young man did not put. A short time after the visit, Buber learned that the young man had died. Realizing that the young man had come to him not for a pleasant chat but for an important decision, Buber was moved to change his view of the "religious". He now saw that the everyday was religious. He saw that the young man who came to him was seeking in Buber "a presence by means of which we are told that nevertheless there is meaning."

I very much like Buber's expression "a presence by means of which we are told that nevertheless there is meaning." This is the type of presence persons should offer to one another. If we did, we would be sacramentals to one another. We would be signs for one another, calls to one another, images of God for one another. Buber wrote:

Each of us is encased in an armour whose task it is to ward off signs. Signs happen to us without respite, living means being addressed, we would need only to present ourselves and to perceive. But the risk is too dangerous for us, the soundless thunderings seem to threaten with annihilation, and from generation to generation we perfect the defense apparatus. All our knowledge assures us, 'Be calm, everything happens as it must happen, but nothing is directed at you, you are not meant, it is just "the world," you can experience it as you like, but whatever you make of it in yourself proceeds from you alone, nothing is required of you, you are not addressed, all is quiet.'[4]

When we meet someone who is present in the way Buber describes presence, "a presence by means of which we are told that nevertheless there is meaning," we meet a holy man. The saints are persons who know how to be present.

The notion of transcendence suggests that persons need never be exhausted or destroyed by the situation in which they find themsleves. Though persons are, they are also *not yet*. A person can always go beyond himself, renew himself, expand himself, transcend his present situtation. The paradox of the personal is that a person comes to exist more deeply and more humanly by dying to himself, by transcending and going beyond the particular moment and situation. A person is a being who is moving toward the future. He is more than either any or all of the facts about him can express. There is a sense in which persons transcend even themselves. This is really what education is all about. Education is supposed to be for the sake of transcendence.

When we say that education is for transcendence, the education experience sounds so exciting. As a teacher, I really believe that education is supposed to help students transcend themselves. Why is it that education so often turns out to be so dull? There are lots of problems: overcrowded courses, dull books, pressure of exams, impatience with the long process of getting a degree — particularly today when there is no guarantee of getting a job through education. More and more reasons could be listed as obstacles to good educational experience. I have no simple solutions to the problems of contemporary education. However, I do think a starting point for all education is to answer the question: "What is supposed to happen to the student?" For me it is as a response to that question that the word transcendence looms large.

Each of us, teachers and students, in whatever level of education we are involved must keep in mind the meaning of what we are doing. Why? To what purpose? What is its value? These are questions we must keep before ourselves. I think that, ultimately, education is what happens between the teacher and the student. The great teacher calls

us, leads us, inspires us. All of us know that there are not many great teachers. However, to have encountered one or two, to have tasted their insight or to have observed their interest and commitment may be enough for us to continue to believe that education is for transcendence. The process of education is a process of opening a person to the world, to reality. I suggest that it is ultimately an opening of a person to God. When human consciousness tastes truth it begins a process that logically leads to Truth. Education is for transcendence. Mindful of Chesterton's insight that anything worth doing is worth doing poorly, I'm very glad I'm a teacher.

Crucial to gaining insight into transcendence is seeing the kind of value that it points to in a person's life. There are problems that are inextricably bound up with the human condition. To be a person is to be plagued by problems that can be described as constitutional to human nature. To be a person is to be a finite being, radically and constitutionally limited. The lives of individuals vary enormously. Some people seem to have not only a larger number of crosses but the worst kind of crosses. Though some may suffer more than others, every adult is going to suffer; every adult lives in the face of death; every adult has to suffer a battle with loneliness and frustration in various forms. Some people escape some problems. No one escapes the problem of being human. Transcendence does not remove human problems. It does, however, introduce values that can transform human problems. It tells

me that in spite of the worst crosses and sufferings, life has a purpose, that reality is gracious, that there is a mystery operative in a person that enables him not only to survive but to grow. Most people call that mystery God.

The notion of response reveals an extremely important dimension of personal existence. For better or worse a person is a responder and responsible.

Whenever it is claimed that people create the meaning of their lives or even that people contribute to the meaning of their existence and their world, some feel that the statements are implying that truth is not objective. Of course, truth is objective but by stressing that a person contributes to the meaning of his vision of life we can focus on the crucial contribution that a person's response makes to the meaning of his existence.

A person is so profoundly a responder that it can be said that this is his nature or his essence. What is a person? He is one who on the deepest level of his being is called to respond. A person is openness to other. By responding, an individual becomes the person he chooses to be. In his response he chooses to be courageous or cowardly, leader or follower, loving or hostile. The way a person responds is extremely influential in the structuring of his world. A person decides to what he will respond and how deeply he will respond.

There is within a person a capacity to choose the meaning of his life, to decide who he is and what his destiny is. Even most "objective" facts can be

interpreted by a person. By the way he focuses his attention, by the emphasis he gives, by his selection of some facts and neglect of other facts or at least by his minimizing the significance of some facts, a person to some extent can structure his world.

If a person is by nature a responder then he is radically at the depth of his being responsible. A person is in charge of his life, in custody of the meaning of his life. A person can be whom he wishes but he must take responsibility for what he does and for the consequence of his actions. That we are responsible for what we do is one of the most important lessons that we must learn.

That persons are responders and responsible becomes crystal clear to me every year in the spring semester. I teach seniors in a college seminary and every spring they must decide whether they wish to go on to the theologate at the major seminary. That a vocation involves a response and that a person is responsible for his vocation becomes quite clear. While each college seminarian can seek counsel and advice from many he finally must make his own decision. He may see more profoundly than previously that he is a responder, that he holds his life in his hands and that he must choose which direction that life will take. Though it reveals our dignity as persons, being responsible can be a burden.

We are ready to vote against all constrictions and inhibitions and ready to sing the praises of freedom but not so ready to affirm the necessary corollary to being free: a person has to answer for

what he freely chooses. What is the world in which I have freely chosen to live? My world is a result of my responses and I am responsible for my world. I must pay for my choices.

A profound insight into human responsibility is present in Arthur Miller's brilliant play *The Price*.[5] Taking place in a late afternoon hour of one day, the play involves Victor, who is a police officer, his wife Esther, and his brother Walter, a highly successful surgeon. The location is the apartment which Victor and Esther had shared for years with Victor's father and to which Victor and Esther have returned for the afternoon in order to clear out some old furniture. Since the father's death sixteen years previously, Victor and Walter have not seen one another. Now they meet in the apartment. Thirty years prior to this meeting, on the occasion of their father's financial failure in the Stock Market Crash, Walter had stormed out of the house, determined to become a successful doctor. Victor decided to forsake the pursuance of a promising career in science in order to take care of his father who was a broken man after the crash. Forced to become a policeman, a job he hated, in order to support his father, Victor has paid the price of his love. However Walter also has paid a price during the last thirty years for his decision: a broken marriage, offspring alienated from him, a mental breakdown and a sense of shame. As the play develops it becomes clear that the father had always been a selfish, penny-pinching man, who could never come to believe that his son Victor would not also walk

out on him. As Walter brings Victor to see this, Victor begins to have doubts about the value of his own life. Trying to explain to Esther and Walter why he spent his life trying to keep his father from disintegrating, he says that his father came home from business after the Crash a beaten man. To the father, everything seemed to be lost, the very meaning of life was in question. Victor's explanation of his commitment to his father is an explanation of his own life commitment and the price he had to pay for it:

> I didn't know what I was supposed to do. And I went out. I went over to Bryant Park behind the library. The grass was covered with men. Like a battlefield; a big open-air flophouse. And not bums — some of them still had shined shoes, and good hats, busted businessmen, lawyers, skilled mechanics. Which I'd seen a hundred times. But suddenly — you know? — I saw it. There was no mercy. Anywhere. One day you're the head of the house, at the head of the table, and suddenly you're shit overnight. . . .
>
> But you're brought up to believe in one another, you're filled full of that crap — you can't help trying to keep it going, that's all. I thought if I stuck with him, if he could see that somebody was still. . . .[6]
>
> I just didn't want him to end up on the grass. And he didn't. That's all it was, and

I don't need anything more.[7]

Victor paid the price for his love. A person is a responder and is responsible.

Personal existence involves relation, presence, transcendence and response. To be free is to relate, be present, transcend and respond freely. All of these aspects of personal existence reveal the dynamic nature of personal freedom. To be a free relational, present, transcending responder is a little like being a lit match in a dark room. Imagine that the dark room is all of reality. A person can penetrate that reality. It depends on the individual how much he sees or knows. Some people spend their lives standing by the entrance of the room. Others have greater interest and experience the excitement of entering further into the room. The person at the entrance is going to have a different vision of the room than the person who explores it in more detail. Many factors contribute to the particular vision of reality that a person has. Though all persons are relational, present, transcending responders, not all persons interpret the meaning of personal existence in the same way. The Christian interpretation of personal existence is unequaled in the dignity it attributes to persons and to loving.

If response is understood in its broadest and deepest possible meaning then it can include within itself the other three characteristics of personal existence: relation, presence and transcendence. Responding can be a way of relating, a way of being

present, and a way of transcending. Using the notion of response to include relation, presence and transcendence, we can say that Christianity calls people to the deepest kind of response. A Christian is responsible even for his faith.

Christianity presents a view of life that is both beautiful and challenging. How much that beautiful and challenging vision actually enters an individual believer's life, however, depends on many factors. The beautiful and challenging vision may be watered down considerably in poor catechisms or superficial religion texts; the vision may be considerably blurred by a slipshod liturgy; the vision may be lost in a poorly prepared or theologically weak homily; the vision may dry up because it has been so long neglected by the individual believer.

These and other reasons can so influence a Christian's faith that his vision of life is more structured by the prevailing non-Christian attitudes and outlooks that surround him than by his Christian faith. To me all this points toward one terribly important truth: believers are responsible for their faith. This truth has to be seen as deeply as possible.

Responsibility in relation to the faith means that people are responsible for the catechism and religion books which appear and are used. Writers have the responsibility to produce the best and Church leaders have the responsibility to use the best. Good religion books don't come about automatically. Someone has to have a faith that

moves him to spend hours composing a good book. Then someone must have the intelligence and foresight to use it.

Responsibility means that both presiding minister and congregation are responsible for the liturgy that occurs any time a Mass is said. We know that ministers can help or hinder, promote or almost prevent a community's participation. As a presiding minister, I can attest to the fact that a congregation's devotion and general interest enormously affect the way I celebrate liturgy. Good liturgy happens because responsible people make it happen.

Though the Gospel is the Good News, the extent to which that news reaches the Christian community depends to a great degree on the homilist. He has a responsibility toward the community. His talent and especially his zeal and faith can help the people in the pews to structure their world around the Christian vision. Responsibility means that the homilist does his job as well as he possibly can.

What needs special emphasis today as such enormous pressures are put on faith is that the individual believer is responsible for his faith. Though God gives the faith and though all sorts of influences affect the faith, the individual believer is ultimately the one responsible for his faith. How does he nurture it? What does he read? How does he pray? How important does he allow his faith to be in his life? How does he allow his faith to be challenged?

One strange but valuable side effect of the pressures that are put on the Christian faith today is

that the responsibility of the individual believer is obvious. No one can believe for someone else. No parent, no friend, no Church can make an act of faith for an individual. A person has to make his own free act of faith. Even God won't take away the individual's freedom. God takes the initiative but man's free response is required. One simple example can illustrate this. A person can freely decide to be present at a Eucharist either attentively and openly or distractedly and in a way that shields him from the Gospel and the challenging dimensions of the Eucharistic celebration. Every time a person opens himself to God's grace he contributes to the growth of his faith-vision; each time he refuses to be receptive to God's grace his faith-vision suffers.

People like to pass responsibility on to others. This human characterisitc holds even in religious matters. What's wrong with the Church? I can blame the Pope, bishops, priests, seminarians and lay people; I can blame collegiality and lack of collegiality, Vatican I or Vatican II, the secularism of worldly men or the narrowness of Churchmen. I tend to blame everyone but myself. Perhaps the most important step for me in answering the question "What's wrong with the Church?" is to look at my faith-vision. What am I doing that prevents Christ from expanding me, from helping me to grow? What am I doing or not doing that prevents Christ from helping me to relate in a Christian way, to be present in a Christian way, to transcend myself in Christian conversion, and to respond fully to God's call?

The difficulties that surround Christian faith today can be the occasion for growth in faith. The pressures upon faith can throw light upon its real nature: a free response to a loving God who calls us to contribute to the making of a new world. Personal existence spells uniqueness. To be a person is to be unique.

Like other personalist philosophers, the French Catholic thinker Emmanuel Mounier stressed that the meaning of a person can never be clearly, concisely or completely expressed. A person can never fit into any fixed, finished or stable category. While persons can be described, Mounier believed that the mystery of a person could not be exhausted by a definition. In a lengthy paragraph in his book *Personalism* (University of Notre Dame Press, Notre Dame, London, 1952) Mounier sees his neighbor, whose name was Bernard Chartier, as an example of the mystery of personhood.[8] He says that he can look at his neighbor's body, examine its dispositions, its heredities, its richness. He can treat his neighbor's body as an object of physical or medical knowledge. He can say that his neighbor is a Frenchman, a bourgeois, a socialist, a Catholic and so forth. Mounier points out, however, that he cannot say that his neighbor is a Bernard Chartier. He is Bernard Chartier. He is a unique person who cannot be captured or capsulized by any external observation or study.

Sketching Greek philosophy's view of man, Mounier then contrasts the Greek vision of man with the Christian vision of person. Stressing that

Christianity's vision of the person was so much more exalted that it was a scandal to the Greek's, Mounier outlines six characteristics of personhood that indicate the Christian contribution to at least one understanding of personal existence.[9] By indicating the six characteristics and briefly commenting on them, I hope to provide a summary of the meaning of personal existence discussed in this chapter.

The first point is that Christianity affirmed the creation *ex nihilo* of each person and his eternal destiny. From the superabundance of God's love, a multiplicity of persons is produced. The love that creates persons and calls them to their goal gives them a unique dignity. There is a humorous expression used often to indicate the uniqueness of an individual. The expression is "When they made him they broke the mold." When God made each person he broke the mold. Persons are precious. Each is fashioned by Omnipotent Love.

The second point is that a person is an indispensable whole. A person is not merely a number of parts put together but is a whole, rooted in the absolute love of God. A way in which we might underline this second point is to say that a person is so special that he is not made for the sake of anything else but rather he is valuable in himself.

The third point is that it is not some abstract Destiny that reigns over persons but God who is himself personal. It is God who offers to each person a relation of unique intimacy. Mounier claims it is a God who affirms himself by granting man a freedom

that is analogous to divine freedom, a God ready "to be generous to the generous." I very much like this last phrase of Mounier's. "Generous to the generous" might be paraphrased as "loving to the loving," or "self-giving to the self-giving."

The fourth point is that the purpose of human existence is to change the heart of its heart (*metanoia*). This change of heart is accomplished by a personal choice. No one but God can judge this choice, this personal transformation which is man's goal.

The fifth point is that a person is freely called to this transformation. God invites man to freely develop his humanity. Essential to the full exercise of man's liberty is the ability to sin, to freely refuse his destiny. God takes man's freedom seriously. The person who is free cannot blame his actions on someone else. A person is made for God, and God wills to be present in love to persons. It must take quite a strong action to dislodge God. Yet a person's freedom is capable of such an action. The fifth point mentioned by Mounier can remind us of the power of freedom.

The sixth point is that the absoluteness of the person neither cuts him off from the world nor from other people. Claiming that the Incarnation confirmed the unity of earth and heaven, of the flesh and the spirit, Mounier believed that persons were created in the image of God and were called to form one immense Body in the charity of Christ. Indicating that the collective history of mankind now made sense, Mounier pointed out that the

revelation of the mystery of the Trinity produced the amazing idea of a Supreme Being who is "an intimate dialogue between persons, and is of its very essence the negation of solitude."

Persons are special. No religion says that more powerfully and beautifully than Christianity. A person can relate, a person can be present, a person can transcend, a person can respond. All these capacities reach their fulfillment in loving.

Discussion Questions on Chapter 2

1. What do each of the four characteristics of the secular spirit mean? Can you give examples of each from your own experience?

2. What is the meaning of relation as a characteristic of personal existence? What are some important relationships in your life? How do they change you?

3. What is the meaning of presence as a characteristic of personal existence? Can you give examples of different ways you are present?

4. What is the meaning of transcendence as a characteristic of personal existence? Can you give examples of yourself either transcending situations or even transcending yourself? Do you ever have the experience of transcending in relation to religion?

5. What is the meaning of response as a characteristic of personal existence? Can you give examples of yourself responding?

6. What is supposed to happen through education?

7. What does it mean to say a believer is responsible for his faith?

8. What are the six characteristics of person which Emmanuel Mounier sketches? Which seems to you to be the most important? Why?

3

Love, Death and Risen Life

Many people look to religion for the wrong reasons or the wrong goals. Perhaps, at times, all of us do. In our calm moments, I think we would agree that the prime function of religion is not to make us feel good or to remove all problems and difficulties from our lives. In our more reflective moments we know this. However, some of us slip back into the attitude that religion not only promises "pie in the sky when you die" but pie right here on earth.

A simple example will illustrate the point clearly. As a priest I have the occasion to attend a large number of wakes. I suspect many parish priests have had experiences similar to my own. It's striking how often the mourners will wonder why the deceased, who was so good and sincere and loving, should suffer and die. Implicit in this reaction to suffering and death is the view that neither suffering nor death should enter your life if you live according to God's laws. However, even a cursory glance through the Gospels suggests that not only is there no evidence for this view but there seems to be evidence for the opposite view. As St.

Teresa suggested, God seems to treat his friends poorly.

No human being is going to remove suffering entirely from his life. Reflection on the nature of personhood and on the nature of suffering suggest that the removal of suffering ultimately might not be in favor of a person's growth. In some strange way suffering can call us to be more human, to reach and activate the depths of our humanity. There are resources in people of which they might never become aware if suffering did not enter their lives. Often people can look back at tragedy or suffering and see that good has come out of it. At the time the suffering is endured or at the time the cross enters a person's life there may seem to be no value to the experience at all. Later, the suffering can be viewed differently. Of course some people can see good and react strongly and courageously even in the midst of tragedy.

The problem of transitoriness or transience becomes more obvious as people advance in age. It seems that nothing human is stable. Nothing endures, nothing lasts. Man's most cherished accomplishments seem to pass away. Civilizations and cultures give way to new human constructions. Daily we grow older. Life seems to be a movement toward death. The seeming transitoriness of all that we experience fills us with insecurity. On what can we rely? On what can we risk our hopes? Is reality, as Shakespeare suggested through one of his characters, "sound and fury signifying nothing"? One of the reasons that death has become such a popular subject with students on all levels of education is contemporary man's heightened sense that all human projects are moving towards death.

In a technological society we are plagued by questions concerning our significance. It's been said that now machines maneuver men rather than vice versa. The question of personal significance becomes pressing. What do I matter? What dent do I make in society? Of what importance to anyone or anything are the few years I spend on this earth? One of the severe problems in contemporary urban life is the problem of loneliness. The experience of loneliness is the experience of personal insignificance, of not being important, of not mattering to anyone.

Because of the pressures placed on us by our experience of life, our religion can be a special help to us. I would describe religion as a totalizing activity, an activity which helps us to "put it all together." Religious vision gives us a sense of where we are and where we're headed. It also helps us to decide in what areas we will put our energies. Religion is deeply related to the transcendent nature of personhood. It might be said that religion is transcendence's thing. Religion is what earthly transcendent beings do. As transcendent beings, we can reflect, evaluate, make decisions, believe, hope and love. Persons are the only beings in our experience who can do this. Persons are the only earthly beings who ask, "Why?" Persons are the only earthly beings who feed on meaning, who probe for and struggle with meaning. Religion can relate to all these human activities. In fact, in a special way, these activities are religion's turf. Religion can help a person get a handle on what bothers him or frustrates him, or on what inspires him or calls him beyond himself. Religion can reveal a person's transcendence to him and help him to explore its meaning and direction. Today this service is more "practical," useful and crucial than much that occupies man in his workaday world. Aimlessness and the atmosphere of disillusion must be conquered. A person has to get some kind of handle on meaning which will illuminate his daily living.

In his essay "Transcendence in Contemporary Piety" in the book *Transcendence* (Richardson and Cutler), Robert Bellah accurately describes the pressing function that the meaning of transcendence can perform if a person is going to move creatively into the future.

> *Somehow or other men must have a sense of the whole. They must have something to believe in and to commit themselves to. Life in its immediacy will not yield to objective analysis, will not wait until all the research results are in. Men must act in the face of uncertainty and unpredictability and consequently they must have faith; they must be willing to take the gamble, the risk of faith. Symbolization of transcendent reality seems inescapable, whether religious in a traditional sense or not.[1]*

It is impossible to overemphasize the value of the symbols and images that lead a person into the future. Such symbols and images either nourish and inspire him or starve and deject him. Though a person can, through transcendence, move beyond crushing images and dead symbols, this is difficult for an individual to accomplish alone. A person is by nature someone who coexists. He needs others. He depends on others not only for his physical needs but for his psychological and spiritual needs. He needs friends to get by, to survive and grow. While a person alone can make a leap of faith beyond what is stifling him and crushing him, he finds it much easier if he is part of a community that is encouraging him, supporting him, calling him into the future, urging him to go beyond himself, beyond his weakness, inertia and fear. A person can thrive and grow in a community that feeds him with transcendent images and symbols. The quotation from Bellah indicates how important religion's role is. If the human community does not have a sense of the whole, a sense of direction or purpose, then human activity will lead to chaos rather than creativity. Rather than subduing the earth, human action will go nowhere.

In the sense in which we are using the word religion, secularism could be called a religion. Though it does not affirm God, it does provide a very strong set of symbols which affects large numbers of people. In spite of signs that there is renewed interest in philosophies of life that include God within their vision, secularism is still a powerful and influential interpretation of reality. Because secularism does affect the consciousness and conscience of Christians, because it does have valuable emphases, and because it provides a good contrast against which the meaning of the Christian vision can be highlighted, a brief sketch of the secularistic worldview may be valuable.[2]

The secularist believes that there is no God. The American secularist, unlike the European existentialist, does not judge that the absence of God makes life absurd. Man, the earth, the galaxies of stars and all the universe are part of one great Nature. Outside of Nature nothing exists. By Nature is meant a complex of matter and energy which is dynamic and self-subsistent. Man is considered to be a product of the evolutionary drive of matter and energy. No further explanation is required for his origin. Evolution is a blind force and could have gone in thousands of other directions but the direction it took produced man. Now that humanity has appeared evolution has become self-conscious. Man is now in charge of its direction. Though he has no goal beyond death, man has many goals on earth. Though he doesn't believe in the doctrine of Original Sin, the secularist sees many evils that should be tackled and thus become part of his life project: to wipe out poverty, to heal the physically and mentally sick, to teach the ignorant, to have a just political and international order and other projects. These are judged by the secularist to be worthwhile goals deserving of his commitment. Probably all the goals which the secularist envisions could be summed up under the all-encompassing goal of the deepest and richest fulfillment of human personality. This goal should not be interpreted in any narrow or selfish way. The secularist wants all persons to be fulfilled, and emphasizes the importance of loving. Ethically there are no absolutes, except the fulfillment of humanity, but the secularist believes this leaves him free to perceive new moral problems and to adjust his ethics to shifting situations. The secularist feels his vision of life is rooted in and based on human experience. His challenge to the Christian is "What of significance does the Christian vision add to the secularist interpretation of human experience?"

The vision of life that a person has colors all his attitudes and activities. It can happen that what is terribly real for one person does not matter at all to another who has a different vision of life. As an example let us imagine a person who is a secularist being asked a question about God. Not only does the person not know the answer but he doesn't even understand the question. The meanings involved in the question are not real or relevant to him. The question is not interesting to him and in no way challenges him. The question is not within his vision of life. To confront the question would involve expanding his vision of life. For the question to be real the person's vision of life would have to change.

Perhaps this last example gives some sense of the importance of a person's vision of life. I suppose in colloquial terminology we would say that a vision of life is "where a person's at." It indicates the outer limits of a person's consciousness, the outer limits of his accepted understandings and values. It is a person's real religion.

What influences our vision of life? I think we can say that everything in our experience has an effect on our vision. Our background, the culture we live in, the books we read, the plays we see, the television we watch, the friends with whom we spend time: all these can contribute to our vision of life. In my own understanding of vision, I stress the importance of freedom. A person's vision of life is influenced by the choices he makes. If I choose to base my understanding of human nature totally on television shows then my vision of life is going to be terribly limited. By spending all my leisure hours watching television serials I enormously limit my vision of life. I don't allow anything to shatter my vision of life, to extend it, to call me beyond it.

If we think of consciousness as openness and presence, we need to see that we direct our consciousness and that we decide to what or to whom we will open ourselves. We freely control our presence. We are not only consciousness but free consciousness and our freedom imposes responsibilities on us. Be open only to the fantasy world of television and your consciousness will be greatly affected. Be present only to the poorest kind of novel and your vision of life will be greatly affected. Approach people only in terms of their function and you will never allow your world to be expanded by the freedom and love that other people can offer you. Close yourself to the mystery that life is and you will be missing a dimension of life that could greatly enrich your personal existence.

Even the slightest reflection on a vision of life indicates the importance that religion can play in a person's outlook. It can extend a person's vision of life enormously. On the other hand the absence of a religious dimension can greatly limit that person's vision of reality. An extreme case is the person who does not even understand religious questions.

One way of looking at friendships and marriages as interpersonal relationships is in terms of two persons' visions of life. When two persons love each other, it can mean that each is saying to the other "Come and see what I see" or "Let me be for you." Probably more than anything else the experience of loving and being loved creates a person's vision of life.

If understood in its broadest meaning, death is the reality which separates the Christian view of life from the secularist vision. Today, because of the pervasiveness and popularity of the secularist vision, special pressure is put on Christians to both articulate and live the significant difference that the Christian mystery makes in their lives. The vision of death that the secularist has can be an incentive for the Christian to translate the Christian vision of death and resurrection into his own life.

It wasn't until about ten years ago while I was doing graduate work in philosophy that I became aware that belief in the immortality of persons was rapidly disappearing among intellectuals. Over the last ten years this impression has become stronger.

When I was a parish priest, I was well aware that no event so tests a Catholic's faith as the death of a loved one. As I attended wakes to console the mourners, I had immediate evidence that nothing could compare to the death event in terms of a person's faith. That evidence was supported by visiting terminal patients in hospitals. Death raised all the important questions.

What surprised me when I started studying philosophy on the graduate level was the number of important thinkers who quickly dismissed the possibility of personal immortality. Some of the thinkers I read claimed that personal immortality was a meaningless belief that hopelessly removed believers from involvement with the problems in this world. For me, contact with such outlooks on death had a kind of reverse spin; it forced me to look at Jesus' resurrection as the central belief of Christianity and to probe what that belief meant to me. The secularistic view of death provides a good example of how the secular vision is a faith, a set of beliefs rather than a set of truths which can be proven. Some vision of death is required if life is to be lived authentically. An individual's view of death profoundly affects his view of life. Philosopher Edith Wyschogrod wrote:

> *As philosophers such as Heidegger, Marcel, and Jaspers have observed, death is not separable from life; if accepted, death provides the standpoint in terms of which life can be lived authentically; if*

evaded it turns life into a charade, a game of lies. To deny that death is that toward which man lives is to treat man as a thing: things merely change, men die.[3]

Our standpoint on death is central to our standpoint on life. Both our standpoint on death and our standpoint on life involve beliefs, acts of faith. Some believe that persons are immortal; some believe that persons are not immortal. The Christian's belief should make a difference in his experience of life.

Of course the Christian vision goes way beyond immortality. Christians do not merely believe that death does not end life; they believe in a new life. The resurrection means a *new* creation. The Christian is meant to experience this new life to some extent now and yet to believe that the experience is just "through a glass darkly" and after death will be "face to face." The experience of the present is different because of Jesus' resurrection; the experience of the future, the experience of the fullness of risen life, will put man's best dreams to shame. The great sign of our share in Jesus' risen life is our love for God and our love for one another. Though that love will reach a fullness and a richness after death, it can be experienced prior to death. St. Paul wrote "And I live now not with my own life but with the life of Christ who lives in me" (*Galatians 2:20*).

There is then a connection between union with the Lord prior to death and union with him after death. The meaning of personal existence can point toward the experience of risen life both now and after death. St. Augustine claimed "God is closer to me than my thoughts." That closeness should color our experience. It should transform personal existence.

Human personality is dynamic and vital. It grows and develops. Human personality is on the move. A person can keep transcending himself, moving beyond where he is, leaving behind his "former self." Ultimately it is because of God's creative presence to a person that he is able to continue transcending himself. Another way of saying this would be that because a person is made in the image of God but will always be an imperfect image, each particular embodiment of that image can be surpassed.

A person has the freedom to transcend himself. But freedom comes to a person as something given. I can exercise freedom to do this or that, to choose A or B, but why should I be free at all? I believe freedom is for the sake of loving. Personal being has a kind of overflow, a kind of superabundance. Is it going anywhere? Is self-transcendence going anywhere? We know it is going toward death but is that all there is to it? I believe that the overflow, the superabundance , and the self-transcendence can go toward loving. Not only can it go toward loving, but it can go toward Love. It is going toward death but death turns out to be the final door toward a new way of loving that is already present and to some extent experienced here and now.

The secularist vision can challenge the Christian to see more deeply into his own faith, his own share in and experience of the Christian mystery. A number of secularist thinkers, if examined closely, could spur the Christian to deepen his reflection on his experience and involvement in the Christian mystery. We will briefly refer to two such thinkers: Friedrich Nietzsche (1844-1900) and Albert Camus (1913-1960). Both thinkers have particular relevance for our reflections because both stressed freedom and personal transcendence. However, they interpreted freedom and personal transcendence in a thoroughly atheistic context. Neither saw how God would add anything to the meaning of human existence. Their interpretation of human experience can challenge us to look and leap further into the Christian mystery. Each thinker can provide a special challenge: Nietzsche because of his originality, enormous influence and complete opposition to Christianity; Camus because of his profound humanism and his enormous popularity today. Each thinker, because of the power of his vision, can call us to confront death and to relate the mystery of resurrection to our daily experience.

Though Nietzsche's view of Christianty can seem extreme, his basic objections are held by many.[4] We Christians continue to appear to many to be weak people who can't face life, people who seek refuge in some other world, people who are waiting for "pie in the sky when they die." In Nietzsche's final philosophical vision of reality courage plays an important role. Nietzsche has been described as a nihilist. For him there was no God and no heaven after death. He claimed that some men would have the courage to face this and he called such men "Supermen." They would be the leaders of the race. He felt that the Superman would come about only if some individuals had the courage to go beyond existing values and morality. Nietzsche felt that the comfort and security provided by existing values and morality were ultimately illusory.

For Nietzsche, Christian morality was an extremely negative morality. He felt that it denied life. The Superman would go beyond this negative morality. He would be the highest development of the race. Besides having strength of will and character, he would be the highest possible development of intellectual power. The Superman would be a person of passion and physique, an independent man, a man of taste. Nietzsche viewed the Superman as a highly cultivated individual. The one thing forbidden to the Superman was weakness. Though tolerant, the Superman would be strong. For Nietzsche, the Superman would be the man who achieved freedom, the man who affirmed life and the world. It is striking how much the Superman seems to be what Nietzsche imagined were the strong but latent powers of the human personality. More than one student of Nietzsche has pointed out that the German philosopher in many ways was the precursor of Freud. Perhaps the genius of Nietzsche was that he perceived some radical needs of human nature even though he came up with a doctrine which really won't fulfill those needs.

Nietzsche's emphasis on courage is also revealed in his doctrine of eternal recurrence. He suggested that each man imagine that his life in its smallest details will recur innumerable times. The man who can face that, the man who can say yes to the eternal recurrence is the man who can say yes to life. He is the courageous man.

In his book *Spoil of the Violent* Emmanuel Mounier meets Nietzsche's emphasis on courage head on and stresses that the Christian must also be a man of courage. Rather than taking a cowardly approach to reality, the Christian must confront it in all its dimensions and immerse himself in the mystery of life more deeply than anyone. Mounier insists that though the Christian must never despair, he must make himself vulnerable to tragedy.

> *Christianity is a stranger to this despair. Is it equally a stranger to tragedy? More often than one likes to admit, one meets under the name of Christianity a code of moral and religious propriety whose chief concern seems to be to discourage outbursts of feeling, to fill up all chasms, to apologize for audacity, to do away with suffering, to bring down the appeals of the Infinite to the level of a domestic conversation, and to tame the anguish of our state.*[5]

I very much like one of the expressions which

Mounier uses, — "to bring down the appeals of the Infinite to the level of a domestic conversation." All of us tend to do this. We shrink God to some image that makes us comfortable so that we don't have to deal with the God who called Abraham into a foreign land, who challenged Moses on Mount Sinai, who asked his Son to die on a cross.

Love can be a terrible thing. It can demand an enormous amount from us. We claim to believe not only that our God loves but that he is Love. If we really believe this then we have to expect surprises and we have to be ready to make sacrifices. Compared to our God and the demands he makes of us, Nietzsche's call for courage doesn't seem demanding. It takes a special courage not to disbelieve but to believe.

French existentialist Albert Camus had a vision of life similar to Nietzsche's, but Camus' tremendous compassion for people makes his view especially appealing. What Camus saw, he saw profoundly. And he wrote about it beautifully. The last page of his highly acclaimed novel *The Plague* can serve as a summary of his vision. Though the plague has subsided, the main character and narrator of the tale, Dr. Rieux knows that it will return. People can't seem to face the absurdity of life but in moments of crisis they rise to the occasion, transcend themselves and courageously face life.

> *...Yes, the old fellow had been right; these people were 'just the same as ever.' But this was at once their strength and*

*their innocence, and it was on this level,
beyond all grief, that Rieux could feel himself at one with them. And it was in the
midst of shouts rolling against the terrace
wall in massive waves that waxed in
volume and duration, while cataracts of
colored fire fell thicker through the darkness, that Dr. Rieux resolved to compile
this chronicle, so that he should not be one
of those who hold their peace but should
bear witness in favor of those plague-
stricken people; so that some memorial of
the injustice and outrage done them might
endure, and to state quite simply what we
learn in a time of pestilence: that there are
more things to admire in men than to de-
spise.*[6]

Is Camus right? Is that all there is? The
Christian thinks not. He experiences life differently,
interprets human experience differently, and should
be willing to risk his life on his faith-interpretation.

We look for signs to help us interpret our
experience but "no sign is given except the sign of
Jonas." The sign that can help us make sense of our
experience is the sign of the Risen Lord. For the
Christian the mystery of the resurrection is a reality
which ought to keep his view of life rich and
exciting. One way to catch the dramatic connection
between the resurrection, understood as including
the entire Paschal Mystery of Incarnation, Death,
Resurrection, Ascension and the presence of the
Risen Lord to the human community, would be to

try to imagine what life would be like without the resurrection. Man's possibilities would be terribly limited. The images that would best characterize life if there had never been a resurrection would be prisons and hospitals, dishonest businessmen and unfaithful marriage partners, violent teenagers and selfish teachers, exhibitionistic entertainment and lustful audiences. Even the resurrection has not so changed life that these images do not apply to much of our experience. However the presence of the Risen Lord among us has made it possible for these images to no longer exhaust or sum up our experience. No longer do these images express all that is possible for man. The resurrection opens up radically new possibilities.

War might be the best image to capture what life would be like without the Risen Lord. War would be normal and natural. How else could we or should we relate to one another? Today many dramatists provide us with images which would exhaust the meaning of man if there was no resurrection. With no resurrection man would be closed, locked in, cut off from the Mystery that animates him, too narrow and sinful to be interested in others, too small to be unselfish and ready to sacrifice.

A few years ago film director Ingmar Bergman put out one of his masterpieces called *Shame*. The film received rave reviews from the critics. In the film Bergman used war as a sign of the way people relate to one another. Bergman seemed to be saying, "Here is what the world is like without God and without love." The images that Bergman used were horrible and the viewer received a vivid impression of how people fail to relate in love. *Shame* could serve as a depiction of what life would be like if there were no resurrection.

Those who think that the resurrection opens new possibilities for people should also realize that people's understanding of the resurrection can expand, grow and deepen. God has become a man and conquered death. We don't understand completely who God is, and the meaning of man is quite mysterious. Both the meaning of God and the meaning of man are dynamic meanings for us.

The more we look at salvation history the more the meaning of God can grow for us. The more we open ourselves to the truths of Scripture, the more the meaning of God can deepen for us. The more real our prayer becomes, the greater the chance that our vision of life will be extended and expanded. To open ourselves to the personal God is to open ourselves, to extend ourselves, to allow ourselves to enter a world that is rooted in the meaning of the resurrection.

All human undertakings can speak to us of man. Literature, theatre, film, poetry, psychology and philosophy are just a few of the avenues that can open up the meaning of man for us. The more concerned with the problems of people we are and the more involved we become the better chance we have of entering into the mystery of being human. The presence of the Risen Lord reveals to us that man is more important and more lovable than we ever could have imagined. The Risen Lord charts new horizons for man. By opening himself to the meaning of God and the meaning of man, by opening himself to the God-man, the Risen Lord, a person opens himself to the meaning of risen life. To miss the meaning of risen life is somehow to miss the meaning of yourself. Jesuit poet Gerard Manley Hopkins expressed this beautifully:

> ...Enough! the Resurrection,
> A heart's-clarion!
> Away grief's grasping, joyless days,
> dejection.
> Across my foundering deck shone
> A beacon, an eternal beam.
> Flesh fade, and mortal trash
> Fall to the residuary worm;
> world's wildfire, leave but ash:
> In a flash, at a trumpet crash,
> I am all at once
> what Christ is,
> since he was what I am, and
> This Jack, joke, poor potsherd, patch, matchwood,
> immortal diamond,
> Is immortal diamond.[7]

By looking at human nature and at ordinary human experience, we can deepen our understanding of Jesus' resurrection. The more meaningful the resurrection becomes, the more light will be shed on human transcendence. My own opinion is that human transcendence and the

76

resurrection are reciprocally illuminative. To probe the meaning of one can shed light on the other. The risen life is the goal toward which human transcendence points.

Human beings spend all their earthly existence in time and space. They place themselves in various vocations and spend their energies in various tasks. A person plays many roles, frequently finds deep fulfillment and frequently encounters frustration. A person has many qualities and can be described in many ways. Because of human transcendence, a person can step beyond all his roles, go beyond all his tasks, and exceed all his qualities. Human transcendence means that man is more than he is at any given moment. A person can be crushed by neither the time period in which he exists, nor by the space which he occupies. Personhood can neither be exhausted nor summed up by any vocation he fulfills nor any task that he tackles. The statement: "Man is more than man" is pregnant with meaning. It suggests that because of consciousness and freedom a person is more than he is at any moment. A person is a strange reality unlike any other reality in our experience. It is a reality whose very nature is to posit itself. Every free choice is a positing of self in a new situation, a new time and a new place. No other reality in our experience can engage in this kind of free self-movement. Personhood is self-creative in the sense that a personal, conscious freedom is never completed, never finished, never final but is always on the move, always relating to changing horizons. There is a sense in which every free choice leads to a new self. A profound free choice can lead to a radical conversion, a dramatic redirection of life, a sudden shifting of goals. The more profound the choice, the more personal; the more personal the act, the more mysterious. The more profound and personal the choice, the more the individual transcends himself.

As a person goes through life transcending his previous states and situations, waiting for him at the end is the experience of death. No matter how meaningful the life, no matter how profound the personal experience, death casts doubt on the significance and value of all human living. The mystery of human transcendence suggests that persons should not die. They do, however. Is there some way that persons can transcend death? The answer is Christ.

That human reality is transcendent is especially clear in the life of Jesus. If you read the various Gospel narratives you discover that Jesus offers us a model of what humanity ought to be. Jesus provides a model for the meaning and form that transcendence should take. A person should keep transcending the time and place in which he exists by moving into more and deeper love relationships. Jesus is the perfect model of humanity. He exemplifies perfectly that which our experience tells us to be true: that love is the direction that transcendence should take.

In dying, and in submitting to his Father's will, Jesus overcame death and thereby demonstrated that love conquers death.

In terms of our own efforts to transcend death by living our life in the presence of the Risen Lord, there is a text from St. Paul that is a classic. Paul tells us that he transcends his past and continues to move toward risen life, toward union with Christ.

If in union with Christ we have imitated his death, we shall also imitate him in his resurrection. We must realize that our former selves have been crucified with him to destroy this sinful body and to free us from the slavery of sin. When a man dies, of course, he has finished with sin.

But we believe that having died with Christ we shall return to life with him: Christ, as we know, having been raised from the dead will never die again. Death has no power over him any more. When he died, he died once for all, to sin, so his life now is life with God; and in that way, you too must consider yourselves to be dead to sin but alive for God in Christ Jesus. (Romans 6:5-11).

The mystery of human transcendence takes on new meaning because of the mystery of the Risen Christ's presence to humanity.

A crisis can play an important role as we try to deepen our experience of ourselves and of Christ. There is a tendency in all of us to get settled, to become accustomed to the way things are, to almost canonize the *status quo*. We like what is familiar and feel uncomfortable with the unknown. We like security and we dread taking risks. In a crisis situation, we tend to question what we have previously assumed and taken for granted. We can be awakened and motivated to look more deeply into the manner in which we are spending our lives. A crisis situation often calls us to go beyond where we are. It can call us to be like Abraham, to leave the familiar and to face the future however fearful it may be. A crisis can make new meanings available for us.

A short story by the late and exceptionally perceptive Catholic writer, Flannery O'Connor, brings out dramatically the force and influence that a crisis can have in helping us to see new meanings and grasp new insights that previously eluded us.[8] The title of the story is *A Good Man Is Hard to Find*. It is particularly interesting because it links crisis with the resurrection. The story suggests that the meaning of Jesus ought to cause a crisis in our lives.

In the story, a family consisting of a young man, his mother, his wife and their three children is taking an auto trip to Florida. Before they leave on their trip, the young man's mother, who in the story is referred to as the grandmother, reads in the newspaper that an insane criminal called The Misfit has escaped from the federal penitentiary and supposedly is heading for Florida. A chronic complainer, the grandmother who does not wish to go to Florida tries to use the story to dissuade her son from the trip. While they are driving to Florida, O'Connor portrays the grandmother as a rather narrow-minded person. During the trip the family is involved in an auto accident and three men stop by, apparently to offer assistance.

As the story develops, it is revealed that the three men are The Misfit and his two accomplices. Through a confrontation between The Misfit and the grandmother, O'Connor illustrates the points that I wish to make: through crises, new meanings can evolve and the resurrection is a meaning which ought to cause something of a crisis in our life.

The Misfit has the members of the family taken into the woods, one by one, and shot until only the grandmother remains. While the other members of the family are being slaughtered, the grandmother tries to engage The Misfit in conversation so that she can persuade him not to kill her. It becomes evident that The Misfit is the way he is because of the way people treated him during his life. He has been created by the meanness and weakness of other people. In desperation the grandmother tells The Misfit to pray and then calls to her son now dead in the woods. The Misfit replies:

> *Jesus was the only One that ever raised the dead. . .and He shouldn't have done it. He's thrown everything off balance. If he did what He said, then it's nothing for you to do but throw away everything and follow Him, and if He didn't, then it's nothing for you to do but enjoy the few minutes you got left the best way you can — by killing somebody or burning down his house or doing some other mean-*

ness to him.[8]

Regreting that he wasn't there at the time Jesus raised the dead (and so is not sure whether Jesus ever did), The Misfit says, "I wisht I had of been there. . .if I had of been there I would of known and I wouldn't be like I am now."

When The Misfit finishes speaking, the grandmother looks at him and says, "Why you're one of my babies. You're one of my own children!" She touches The Misfit's shoulder and he, frightened and repelled by this sign of affection, shoots her. Walking away from her dead body and replying to an accomplice's comment that she talked too much, The Misfit says that she would have been a good woman if there had been somebody there to shoot her every minute of her life.

My interpretation of the story is that The Misfit is the product of a sinful society. The grandmother for all her talk of prayer never really confronted the Christian meaning of brotherhood. At a moment of crisis, when she is facing death, she sees that Jesus' actions and resurrection implicate us in each other's lives. Some of the meaning of Jesus dawns on the woman as she faces death.

The meaning of Jesus can open new worlds and horizons for people. The resurrection is the love-explosion. The meaning of Jesus ought to cause a crisis in peoples' lives. The Misfit is right: if Jesus did what he said, there's nothing to do but throw away everything and follow him."

Discussion Questions for Chapter 3

1. How can suffering help us to grow? Can you give any examples from your own life?

2. How does your religion help you "to put it all together"? How does your religion give you a sense of your transcendence?

3. What are the main ideas in the religion of secularism? Can you attest to the influence of secularism in your life?

4. How would you describe your vision of life? What most influences your vision of life?

5. Why is death a good topic for contrasting the secularist and Christian visions of life?

6. What is Nietzsche's view of courage? What is Mounier's?

7. What is transcendence for Camus?

8. Can you point to experiences in your own life that would be radically different if there was no resurrection and no risen Lord present in your life?

9. Can you point to any deeper or better understanding of the resurrection you have received recently?

10. In Flannery O'Connor's story a crisis leads to a deeper insight into the meaning of resurrection. Can you give any examples from your own experiene of crisis leading to a deeper understanding of resurrection?

4

Love and Co-Existence: Personal and Christian

Personal growth is filled with paradox. Often that which seems to be antithetical to personal growth, for example sacrifice and suffering, is what is most favorable to personal growth. Problems and trials are occasions for people to transcend themselves, to progress to a new level of existence, to become more deeply persons. Philosopher Robert Johann expressed this well.

> *Man is not merely an individual nature looking for its own fulfillment; he is a person summoned by love. He is called not to comfort but to creativity; not to satisfaction but to service. The price of such service runs high; it involves even death. But the stakes are higher still — they involve God Himself.*
>
> *Beyond our joys and griefs, therefore, what God wants is our hearts, our utter devotion and love. In the light of this love if we truly live it, suffering itself is transfigured.[1]*

Christianity is filled with paradox. When Christians claim that God is the Father of man they should realize the he is a Father who often asks a great deal of his children. He asked Jesus to die. I think there is a sense in which he asks each of his sons to die. The process of growing in sonship seems to be at least partially a process of dying. The expression "by dying we live" sums up the kind of existence that involvement in the Christian mystery demands. No one welcomes either suffering or death. Yet we learn that somehow when suffering is endured and death is confronted we can live in a new way, a way that is more profoundly personal, a way that is rooted in a meaning of which we were previously unaware.

We have to remember that neither persons nor God are static beings. The relationship between two persons is a dynamic, developing reality. It can intensify or weaken, deepen or grow shallow, liberate or constrain, inspire or depress. The relationship is similar to the relationship between a person and God. The crucial difference is that the relationship between a person and God will never weaken, grow shallow, constrain or depress because of any weakness or lack on the part of God. The God in whom Christians believe is the One who is always trying to intensify the personal existence of man, to liberate man from the narrow and constricting elements that block his growth, to inspire man to courage and love. To believe in such a God is to involve yourself in mystery. It is to open yourself to the unexpected, to relate yourself to a Love that is so powerful that it is identical with a Person.

We really don't understand God's providence. I don't know the details of God's plan for me. Every time I try to formulate it, I realize that I create an idol, a blueprint made more in my own image and likeness than in the image of the Almighty. When I try to conceive of the mystery of providence, I must start with the truth that I don't completely understand God. I can't fit God into my head. As St. Thomas aptly pointed out, while we know that God is we don't know what God is. God goes beyond all our images and ideas. He escapes all our concepts and eludes all our formulations. When we deal with him we deal with mystery.

The importance of loving in Christian existence is more clear if emphasis is placed on the communal nature of personhood. The way that some contemporary philosophers express this communal nature is by saying that to be a person is to co-exist. What many contemporary thinkers see is that for an individual to be human he needs other humans. For me to be me, I need you. By emphasizing the contemporary insight into co-existence we can see how easily a Christian can drown in a secular culture. We may also be able to see a wonderful aid that could help him to survive.

A person needs other persons on the biological and physical levels. Even on these most basic levels, persons co-exist. An individual cannot survive alone. A person is given life through the action of two other people. A child is sustained in life by the care and concern of others. For a number of years the physical survival of a child depends on the kindness of others.

I've heard stories about children who were lost as infants and who grew up among animals. To imagine what such a child would be like is to see how persons depend on one another for growth. Such a child would act like an animal. Because he had not co-existed with humans, such a child would be, to say the least, uncultured. He might be vicious. Since no humans taught him how to behave he would be, to a large extent, trapped on the animal level.

The meaning of co-existence on the physical level goes far beyond the early years of one's life. In contemporary cutlture we are locked together by a long chain of interrelationships. If one link in the chain breaks, many suffer. An obvious example was the gas crisis, a couple of years ago. I heard a number of people make statements similar to "My whole life changed because of the difficulty of obtaining gas." I found myself planning my day around the amount of gas I had in my car. In our culture co-existence on the physical level is obvious.

Even more important than co-existence on a physical level is co-existence on the level of thought. When we see how deeply we co-exist on the level of thought, insight, and meaning, we can see how much our culture forms us. From a person's earliest years he is given meaning from sources outside himself. A "world-already-interpreted" is handed to him. As a child he is told what to eat and what not to eat, what to touch and what not to touch, what to do and what not to do. A child is told what is true and what is false by his parents. Psychologists tell us that parents play an enormous role in forming the image of God for their children.

This process of receiving a "world-already-interpreted" continues through much of school. Somewhere this should stop. As a teacher, I suspect that for some people it never stops. They never learn to question, to freely agree or disagree. In my opinion the process of education has failed for such people, no matter how many degrees they hold.

This imposition of meaning continues after school. Our culture tells us what to think of the poor, of blacks of women, of religion and, indeed, of just about everything. To disagree with your culture isn't easy. To be a Christian alone is impossible. To exist as a Christian in a secular culture is rough. One way to avoid drowning is to emphasize Christian co-existence, to get a little help from your friends.

There is among the Vatican Council statements one that is particularly provocative in relation to the question of Christian co-existence. The Council Fathers stressed that the living conditions of modern man have so changed that it is legitimate to speak of a new age in human history. New avenues have opened up in social sciences and technology, and modern man has means of communication which were unavilable in previous periods. The Council Fathers wrote:

> *In every group or nation, there is an ever-increasing number of men and women who are conscious that they them-*

*selves are the artisans and the authors
of the culture of their community.
Throughout the world there is a similar
growth in the combined sense of in-
dependence and responsibility. Such a
development is of paramount importance
for the spiritual and moral maturity of the
human race. This truth grows clearer if we
consider how the world is becoming
unified and how we have the duty to build
a better world based upon truth and
justice. Thus we are witnesses of the birth
of a new humanism, one in which man is
defined first of all by his responsibility
toward his brothers and toward history.*[2]

The thrust of the quotation from this Vatican II
statement is that culture is somehow due to the
activity of people. In its most radical structures, its
most basic roots, a culture may be tied to the nature
of persons. I suspect that it is. However in its
particular shapes and forms, in what distinguishes it
from other cultures, a particular culture is very
much due to the activity of people. One way of
describing a person is to say that he is a builder of
culture. Only persons build cultures. Animals, while
they have set patterns of activity, do not have
cultures. It would seem ludicrous to say an animal is
cultured. The word "culture" suggests something
specifically human. I suggest that culture is tied to
cultus, that a culture reveals what a person worships
and holds precious. A culture reveals what people

love.

Reflection on the quotation from "The Church Today" can cause both excitement and a certain anxiety. The world is shrinking and we have new opportunities to grow to maturity. However, the new opportunities bring new responsibilities. Can we meet these responsibilities? Will we meet these responsibilities? It's possible that we may miss the moment. The more we think about religion and culture the more important the relation between the two becomes.

There are many definitions of culture. I don't know if there is any one definition that is totally satisfactory. I could list a number of different definitions that sociologists use but I don't think such a list would be particularly valuable for my purposes. In a more scholarly treatment such a list would be a necessity. For my purposes I'm going to use as a working definition, "A culture is the outward expression of a person or a group of persons striving to become what they think they should be." I am well aware of the broadness of this definition. The reason I choose it is that I want to provoke as much thought as possible and I'm hoping that the broadness of the definition will provide an umbrella effect. As I'm using the word, a culture includes most of what goes on in an individual's life. I want to consider a culture as both the outward expression of a community and the outward expression of an individual. There is an American culture and there is also what might be called a "Bob Lauder culture." Neither is easy to describe accurately, though the latter is probably easier to describe than the former. Each individual has a culture which is not quite identical with the culture of the various groups to which he belongs. If an individual sees some area of his life in which he wishes to improve his taste he might describe his need as a "need to get some culture." He might join a book group, or a theatre group or make arrangements to attend the opera or the ballet regularly with some of his friends. Looking at my own taste and interests, I am well aware that the opera world is rather foreign territory to me. The few times that I have attended the opera I have left whistling the score of "My Fair Lady." I'm not proud of my opera deafness and with the encouragement of my friends I may do something to allow opera to humanize me. The point I wish to stress is that the arts play a large role in an individual's culture.

In addition to the arts, your ethnic background, home atmosphere, the schools you attended, your neighborhood, state and country all play a role in forming your individual culture.

A culture is built by people but the culture also sort of doubles back and imposes itself on people. The larger the group the more complicated an individual's cultural life can be. For example, parents of a family may try to create a cultural life for their four children. As the children grow their parents' genuine interest in literature and poetry, painting and music is communicated to them. All the children receive from their parents a lively interest in, and a taste for, the arts. The world of the family is enriched by this exposure to the arts. We are not considering the particular ethnic background of the family and the distinctive traits which the children might receive if the parents were of Irish, Italian or Jewish background. We are limiting our example to the arts. The parents try to create a particular type of culture for their children.

However, the family doesn't live in isolation. The children mix with other children, attend schools, go to movies, join the mainstream of American life. A culture that was not created by this particular family is now imposed on it or at least the family is forced to engage in a dialectical relation with the larger culture. To consider that dialectical relation between the larger group, the country for example, and a smaller group, the family, can be a simple way of seeing the problem of the relation between religion and culture.

Suppose the cultural life created by the family is nourished by the cultural life of the country? This is a marvelous experience. The family sees that it needs help. Educators, artistis, writers and television people aid it. John Donne's famous line "no man is an island" has a rather joyous ring to it when the family's cultural life is supported, aided and deepened by the larger group's cultural life. However, suppose it goes the other way? Suppose the larger group's cultural life is almost antithetical to the family's cultural life? Suppose the family feels that the larger group's cultural life is impoverished? Suppose the family judges that the relation between itself and the larger groups will only cheapen the family, encourage the family to lose its taste? Now "no man is an island" is frightening. Now apply the example from the arts to values and morals and ideas about God. What does a religion do if it judges that the culture in which it exists not only fails to support it but works against it? The problem of religion and culture is no small problem.

One of the key insights that we must have into co-existence is that culture is built by persons. Though I may be born into a particular culture and in this sense a culture is "given" to me or imposed on me, some person or group of persons created the culture I inherit. Culture is the product of persons. If we think of a large culture such as the American culture, we realize that a number of influences go to make it up.

Religion is the most influential factor in a culture. By religion in this context I don't mean an institutional organization. For example, in our American culture at this time institutional religion doesn't seem to have much clout. Many commentators consider institutional religion to be in a state of crisis and near collapse. When I claim that religion is the prime force in molding a culture I mean religion as a life stance or as an ultimate system of meaning. What dictates the face, form and style of a culture is the life stance (religion) that people take. By religion I don't necessarily mean a form of theism. I mean a worldview that may be agnostic or even atheistic. A culture reveals what is finally important to the community. A culture reveals what people love.

In the complicated society and sets of communities in which we live, it is not easy to localize the people who create a culture. Who are the thinkers, the power people, the leaders who make a difference? Is the life stance or reliion of the American community really the life stance of the majority of the people or is it the stance of a few who have a great deal of influence? My impression is that the power is in the hands of a few. Those who run the media make an enormous contribution to the culture in which we live. Though it might be argued that the media manipulators need an audience, the power of the media is such that it can almost create its audience. The power of the press is enormous; that television has a tyranny over us is not a baseless fear.

I suggest that even behind the power of the media is religion. A worldview or a vision of life leads those who run the media to put forth the images and values which they present. I almost agree with Karl Marx that the most powerful reality in the world is an idea. What has to be discovered is the vision of life upon which a culture is built. That is what is crucial. Whether the vision of life is held by an entire community or only by the educators or only by the media people is a secondary question. The vision of life with or without God is the religion that forms a culture.

One example from history will illustrate the importance of the point I'm trying to make. Almost one hundred years ago the German philosopher

Friedrich Nietzsche declared that God was dead. What Nietzsche meant was that the culture in which he lived was trying to support a view of God that no longer fit the self-understanding of many people. Nietzsche wrote:

> God is dead. God remains dead. And we have killed him. How shall we, the murderers of all murderers, comfort ourselves? What was holiest and most powerful of all that the world has yet owned has bled to death under our knives. Who will wipe this blood off us? What water is there for us to clean ourselves? What festivals of atonement, what sacred games shall we have to invent? Is not the greatness of this dead too great for us? Must not we ourselves become gods simply to seem worthy of it? There has never been a greater deed; and whoever will be born after us — for the sake of this deed he will be part of a higher history than all history hitherto.[3]

What Nietzsche was claiming was that a vision of personhood had emerged which no longer supported belief in God. An atheist, Nietzsche did not believe that there was a God who literally died. What the German philosopher was claiming was that people had so come of age, had so matured that they could no longer retain the childish conception that there was a God who created people and watched over them.

The quotation from Nietzsche brings out rather dramatically the problems of the relation between religion and culture. What Nietzsche was claiming was that one culture which was built up by a religion (Christianity) was now dead. He was arguing that a new religion (atheism) had to create a new culture. Were people up to that task? Could they do it? Would they have the courage to do it?

Today the situation in this country is difficult for those who believe in Christ. I think our culture is underlined by a worldview that is secular. How can those who believe in Christ dialogue with that culture? Can belief in Christ survive? Can it be translated into a day-to-day living? These and similar questions are testing the faith of many.

In order to see that religion is the basis of culture we have to see that every person has a religion, that every person is a believer. Obviously, I am not using the word "religion" to indicate an institutional worshipping community nor am I restricting the word "believer" to those who affirm God. However, what I am trying to stress goes far beyond the pleasantries of a word game or a dispute over semantics. Words can trap us into thinking along fruitless lines and lock us into fixed patterns of judging. What I am stressing is essential if Christians are going to see the traps and pitfalls that surround them in a secular culture. Once the Christian realizes that everyone has a religion, that everyone, even the atheist, is a believer, the Christian can breathe a new air and develop a more accurate outlook on his culture.

We'll treat the meaning of religion first. Everyone has a religion in the sense that everyone has a worldview or a life stance. Every person has some kind of ultimate view, some set of values by which he lives. Some may have difficulty articulating their point of view but that doesn't mean that they don't have one. Some people may never reflect on their worldview but that does not indicate that they don't have one. Some people may frequently shift their point of view or have one that is not totally consistent. In relation to my thesis this doesn't matter. Such people still have a religion though they may never refer to it as a religion. Their worldview or life stance and their set of values go to make up their religion. Whatever tag or title persons give their basic approach and outlook of life, that approach and outlook go to make up their religion.

Some people may describe their general attitude toward life as "hanging loose." To the extent that their description of their attitude is accurate, then their religion is the religion of hanging loose. That's their worldview; that's their stance on life. This is the attitude they have toward the world, toward reality. Hanging loose is a catch phrase under which they fit their beliefs and values. If a person claims, "I don't accept any dogmas" then to the extent that this is an accurate description, his religion is "no acceptance of dogmas."

The meaning of belief is closely related to the meaning that I am applying to religion. To say that every person has a religion is implicitly to say that every person is a believer. No one can prove his stance on reality. This is not to say that all stances, outlooks or attitudes on reality are equally reasonable, or equally unreasonable. It is to say that no matter how much evidence a person can muster up to defend his position or to support his worldview, he cannot prove his worldview. He cannot so establish it that every person who sees his argument must accept it and must affirm that position. Essential to all worldviews is an act of faith, and act of belief. In this sense the choice of a worldview entails going beyond the evidence. Every time a person accepts or affirms a worldview he makes an act of faith. He becomes a believer. And every person is a believer.

Why make such a point of this? Why all the fuss? The reason is that in America, today, Christians exist in a secular culture. This means that the predominant beliefs that surround me not only do not support my Christian belief but actually work against it. Once I know that a secular society is rooted in secular beliefs rather than in facts or proofs or self-evident truths, I can achieve a new freedom in relation to my own belief. In a secular culture I can be threatened by worldviews that oppose my own. Without realizing it I can begin to think that "fifty million Frenchmen can't be wrong," that the truth must be what the majority holds, that the facts and the evidence are all against me. Once I realize that the secular outlook is a religion, a set of beliefs then I can measure my own set of beliefs against it rather than half-consciously feel that I live in a fantasy world and the secularists live in the real world.

Today, in our society, it is difficult to be a Christian believer. I don't mean that it is difficult to mouth pious platitudes about Christ. Anyone can do that. I mean that to really believe, to make a personal commitment to Christ that makes a difference in your life is difficult. I'm sure it always has been. The particularly contemporary burden is that American culture in many ways tells the Christian believer that his belief is meaningless. Perhaps to believe in Christ in such a culture requires that a person be a kind of martyr (one who bears witness). To realize that the culture is rooted in a set of beliefs relieves a little of the pressure of bearing witness.

A particular burden that is placed on loving in our society is the pressure put on us to use one another. We tend to reduce one another to our functions. The Jewish religious thinker Martin Buber had provocative insights into this problem. He claimed that there are two basic ways of relating: I-It and I-Thou. Buber claimed that all relationships could fit under one of these two headings. Though his ideas about I-It and I-Thou are fairly well known, and though the ideas have become so popularized that the terms are used in everyday conversation by people who have never read Buber, I think another look at I-It and I-Thou can be profitable. Buber's insights into relationships are so valuable that every time we study his I-It and I-Thou categories we can expand our understanding of the meaning of personhood. Though I-It is less important we can, by reflecting on it, begin to sense the value of an I-Thou relation. We will discuss the I-Thou relationship in the next chapter.

An I-It relationship is a pragmatic, functional relationship.[4] A person relates to the other, whether it be an object or a person, only in terms of the other's function. In effect, the person addresses the other with the question, "What can you do for me?" or "What can I use you for?" A simple example can illustrate the meaning of an I-It relation. Let me use the example of my relationship with my car. Even though, when I buy a car, I spend some time choosing the color and the accessories, my main interest is whether the car will function with a minimum amount of difficulty. Will the car get me where I want to go? Will it do the job I want it to do? I really don't care what the car looks like (anyone who has seen it will agree). I really don't care about the model. I really have no attachment to *this* car rather than to some other car. I want it to function properly. With my car, I have an I-It relation.

What is particularly interesting about an I-It relation is that it is a superficial realationship. I don't focus in on the uniqueness of the "It." The object or person is just one of many. To me the object is a type, a member of a class, rather than a unique individual. I don't focus deeply on the mystery of the other. I only know *about* it, what it does, how it works. From the point of view of grasping the "It," and I-It relationship is superficial.

Equally important for an understanding of Buber's insights is that from the point of view of the "I," an I-It relationship is superficial. Nothing is asked of me in an I-It relationship. I do not relate profoundly. I give very little of myself. I am not deeply transformed by an I-It relation. My car asks little of me. Driving the car demands a minimum amount of attention. After driving the car, even after a long trip, I am pretty much the same person I was before I drove it.

To catch the significance of this, we have to imagine a person who has multiple I-It relationships and few, if any, I-Thou relationships. Such a person has little opportunity to grow. He is living superficially, relating only functionally. Perhaps he is extremely proficient at I-It relationships. His efficiency may even be making him a fortune. Still he is growing very little as a person.

Buber pointed out that no one can survive without I-It relationships, but if an individual has only I-It relationships, then he is not a person. To me this is very interesting. What Buber is saying is that it is not to what or to whom you relate that matters, but *how* you relate that counts. In other words, you might be relating to some marvelous people, but you may be treating them as "Its." If so, then none of the richness of their personalities will affect or influence you. The other person is an "It" to you because that's the way you stand in relation to him. You will not allow him to be a "Thou." There is a double tragedy here. First, you box him in and you won't allow him to grow through your gift of self. By withholding yourself and treating him as an object, you rob him of the richness of your person. Secondly, you cheat yourself. If to you he is only an object, then you are only a user of objects. You prevent yourself from experiencing the unique way of growing that comes about by giving yourself to another person. The pace of contemporary living encourages us to multiply I-It relationships. In multiplying them, we may become proficient at them. The danger is that we will forget how to relate in an I-Thou relationship. We may start treating a person as an "It." This seems to be a kind of a sacrilege.

Love always focuses on the uniqueness of the other. Though when Buber's notion of the I-Thou is considered in the next chapter, we may judge that it is such an exalted relationship that the ideal of having it with every person we meet is a bit unreal, we can strive never to reduce a person to an "It." We can also strive to have at least a minimal loving attitude toward all persons. There are levels of love. I love members of my family in one way, my closest friends in another way, the people to whom I minister in another. Love has many faces and degrees. To love is to refuse to reduce a person to his or her function and to be in favor of the person's growth. Love means "I am for you." There can be various ways of making a self-gift. With some people I love, I spend a large portion of my life; with others I may spend only an hour. What is crucial is the self-gift.

That a person co-exists means that a lover must

be interested in the social structures which either help or hinder people in loving one another. Love is never private. This is ultimately why the Church has a social doctrine. The Church must be concerned that the way people co-exist in society aids rather than hinders their experience of the Christian mystery.

Throughout my adult life I have been interested in the Church's social doctrine. Unfortunately that doctrine is rarely communicated well. What might be called private or personal morality has been communicated very well: every Catholic knows about the sinfulness of lying, cheating, impurity, stealing. Both moral teaching and the experience of private confession have contributed, each in its own way, to the formation of the Catholic conscience and to both the strengths and weaknesses of that conscience. While the Church has a strong social doctrine, and a collection of marvelous encyclicals on social justice, that doctrine is not easily translated into concrete terms. There are of course a whole group of Catholics who are not aware that the Church has a social doctrine. If a priest gives a homily on some aspect of the Church's teaching such as racial prejudice, then it's a good bet that some of the congregation are going to complain that the priest is talking politics. Some people don't see any conflict between reception of the Eucharist and racial bigotry. Regular reception of the Eucharist and prejudiced attitudes toward some group or groups can co-exist with no apparent conflict of conscience, even among people who have had a good deal of formal Catholic education.

The difficulty with Catholic social teaching goes even further. Many who know of the existence of Catholic social doctrine and who have read the encyclicals still can't translate that teaching into concrete day-to-day examples. This situation was brought home to me again when I read a provocative chapter on "critical theology" in Gregory Baum's latest book *Religion and Alienation*. Baum has focused on the problem of social morality in an exciting but complex way.

In his discussion of personal and social sin, Baum describes critical theology:

> *It is the task of critical theology to bring to light the hidden human consequences of doctrine, to raise the consciousness of the believing community in this regard, and to find a manner of proclaiming the Church's teaching that has structural consequences in keeping with the gospel.*[5]

Baum stresses that all belief, all doctrine has hidden consequences and that the way belief is proclaimed has all sorts of structural consequences. He continues:

> *In the case of Christology this means that a way of announcing God's Word in Jesus must be found which does not devour other religions but actually makes room for the multiple manifestation of*

*God's grace. There is not a single doctrine
of the Church, nor a single aspect of spirituality, worship or Church life that may be
exempted from a critique that distinguishes between intention and structural
consequences and evaluates the latter
in terms of the gospel.*[6]

While Catholic consciences have been sensitized
toward personal sin, they have not been sensitized to
sinful situations that are due to certain structures
within both society and the Church. Critical
theology focuses on the structural consequences of
belief apart from the good or bad intentions of those
holding the belief. The example that Baum
emphasizes is the privatization of the Gospel, the
overly individualistic interpretation of the Christian
message. Looking at the work of Jesus as the
salvation of souls rather than the bringing in of a
new age has all sorts of implications. Those
proclaiming that Jesus came to save souls may have
the best intentions in the world but they, perhaps
quite innocently, are shrinking the Gospel message.
If I believe that Jesus came to save souls then my
religion seems doomed to become a "me and Jesus"
activity, I will neither expect to see signs of the
kingdom of God in the world nor work toward
bringing about that kingdom. I will work toward my
own salvation but I won't be terribly concerned
about either social or ecclesiastical institutions, or
about social or ecclesiastical structures. I just won't
think of such realities in relation to salvation. If I

believe Jesus came to save souls, I will think of myself as a sinner but the concept of a "sinful Church" probably will mean little to me. I may presume that the Church and the kingdom are the same. It's more likely that I don't think much of the kingdom because my notion of salvation will be too individualistic.

To be critical of institutions is not easy. Many of us tend toward one of two extremes: we naively accept the institution or we are overly critical. What Baum is after is criticism in light of the Gospel. The new penitential rite emphasizes the social nature of all sin. The entire rite calls the attention of the penitent to the truth that personal sin affects the community. Baum has taken us one step further by pointing out that there can be sinful structures even when no individual is guilty. To criticize institutions and societal structures is very difficult but it's a necessary task if we are interested in the kingdom of God.

The complexity of social structures is probably the main reason that criticism of social structures is difficult. Probably most Christians are in favor of helping the poor but how is this to be done? Christians are in favor of promoting racial justice but how to promote it is the question. Christians are opposed to dehumanizing social structures but how can they change them? One obvious way to help the poor is through almsgiving. While almsgiving can be encouraged, it is grossly inadequate if an injust social structure is promoting poverty. One way of helping to bring about social justice is through consciousness-raising. I don't think the good that can be done through consciousness-raising should ever be minimized. Great movements often begin with consciousness-raising. It is no small thing to change someone's mind, to help someone begin to think in a new way. However consciousness-raising is a minimal response if the structures of society are promoting racial injustice. Dehumanizing structures can work against all the best will in the world. The task is to find where the sickness lies in a society and to attack it directly.

What often makes criticism of social structures difficult is that the would-be critic may be part of the structure. To rise above a situation, to be able to get a perspective on a structure is especially difficult for the person who is immersed in the situation under scrutiny. This seems to be a particular problem for a member of the Church. Many Catholics think that criticism of the Church amounts to a kind of betrayal or treason. If the Church is perfect in all its aspects then all adverse criticism of the Church is wrong. But the Church is not perfect in every aspect. The Church is not identical with the kingdom of God. Karl Rahner has written:

> ...*a critique of the Church in the name of the Church is always possible because her own understanding of her own nature is always wider, freer, and more exalted than that which is **de facto** realized in the form which she assumes in history, and is in fact wider in scope than that which we*

have already formulated to ourselves about her at the level of speculation and theory.[7]

What Rahner is saying is that the Church is always capable of growth, always capable of being better than she is at any moment, always capable of being a better sign of God's kingdom. If Catholics believe this, then they not only can but should engage in responsible criticism of some aspects of the Church's existence. Such criticism will spring from faith and love. Its goal will not be to tear down and destroy but to build up and perfect.

Criticism of other structures by a Catholic can also be difficult. Catholics are so accustomed to the absolute truth of dogma that they often don't feel at home with the less absolute thinking that is required in dealing with matters of society. Every Catholic is in favor of racial justice but what does that mean in a concrete situation? Every Catholic wants the poor to be helped but what kind of obligations does that place on individual Catholics?

In 1976 an individual Catholic gave tremendous witness to the social teaching of the Church. Carmelite Bishop Donal Lamont was found guilty by the Rhodesian government of endangering Rhodesian national security. Bishop Lamont had told a young nun to give medical supplies to some freedom fighters who had requested them. Bishop Lamont reported his conversation with the nun as follows: "Look when people come looking for medical help, you give it.

You don't ask political affiliation, you don't ask what their religion or anything else is. You have a Christian obligation to give them medical help." He then told the nun, "I will take full responsibility. If the authorities say, 'Did you not report this,' say 'The Bishop told me not to, and I will be responsible.'"[8] Lamont believed that he had no obligation to report those who were seeking aid though he knew what the legal consequences would be for him. The Rhodesian court sentenced the bishop to ten years in prison. Because he was opposed to the racism in Rhodesia Bishop Lamont, who was eventually expelled from the country, was ready to suffer imprisonment. Here is a concrete example of a Christian making an enormous personal sacrifice because he believes a social structure to be immoral.

Each of us can fantasize about the good work he or she might do for Christ. We can imagine ourselves capable of all sorts of self-denial. How capable are we? Would I be ready to go to prison? Bishop Lamont in a dramatic and heroic way provided criticism of a social structure. In describing his action of taking responsibility for giving the medical supplies he said, "I was just doing what had to be done." The good bishop disturbs my conscience. I hope more of us can be the kind of witness to Christian love that he is.

When we realize how much we influence one another for better or worse on all levels of our life, the importance of Christian community looms large. We do co-exist on all levels of life: physical, psychological, personal. We also co-exist spiritually. In God's providence, he has arranged that salvation should come through a community. If I am going to be a Christian, I need other Christians. My faith needs your faith. Your hope and trust encourages me to hope and trust. Your Christian love life can affect my love life. We come to be Christians through the Christian community.

Of course the primary Christian community has to be the Church and the primary activity which unites Christians has to be the Eucharist. Through the Eucharist we find out who we are, we find our Christian identity. In worshipping God and in affirming our sonship, we also find our brotherhood. One reason why the liturgical revival and renewal is so terribly important is that it helps us to co-exist as Christians more profoundly. Every sacrament leads us to a deeper co-existence with other Christians. There are no private sacraments; each has a community orientation.

The four moments of love — call, free response, fulfillment of the lover, and creative freeing of the beloved — are moments that are supposed to be happening all the time in the Christian community. Every member of the Christian community is a call, a need and an appeal to other members. Love is a free response to that call or need. The member who loves says in effect "I am for you, I am available to you, I want you to grow, to fully embrace Christ who has embraced us." When a member responds by loving, that member is fulfilled in a new way. In loving, the member discovers that the pattern of

Christ's death and resurrection is repeated in him through his gift of love to others: the lover discovers that through dying he lives; through giving himself away, he increases; through being unselfish, he becomes a renewed Christian self. The member who is loved can be created by the one who loves. The member of the Christian community who experiences the love of the other members for him can become a new "Christian you." The love he experiences opens new possibilities for him. When the four moments of love are present in the Christian community, it means that the members of the community are making themselves through God's grace into a better image of Christ, a more alive and attractive sign of Christ's presence, a more clear sign of profound truth that they are the Body of Christ. St Augustine's lovely description of the Church comes to mind: one Christ loving himself.

Today there are a number of movements within the Christian community which are thriving and which underline the importance of Christian coexistence. The Marriage Encounter, the Cursillo, the Christian Awakening, the Charismatic Prayer Movement are a few examples. In each of these movements the importance of Christian coexistence is clear. The members experience a need for a close-knit, more intimate experience of Christian brotherhood within the larger community that is the Church. In each of these movements, and in other similar movements, the members can be profoundly affected through the Christian co-existence they experience. This Christian co-existence, the presence of love the members experience within the Christian community, should move them in love and service toward the wider human community. Love never narrows us or closes us in on ourselves. Love is a dynamic which ought to continually extend itself toward more and more people. This is especially true of Christian love. Like his Risen Lord, the Christian counts all others as his brothers and sisters.

Discussion Questions for Chapter 4

1. How is suffering transfigured through love? Can you give an example from your own life?

2. What does it mean to say persons co-exist? Can you offer examples of co-existence from your own experience?

3. What did the Council Fathers mean by "the birth of a new humanism"? Can you cite signs of this new birth from your own experience?

4. The author has described culture as "the outward expression of a person or a group of persons striving to become what they think they should be." What has influenced your own personal culture? What influences American culture?

5. How has culture affected your religion?

6. What in American culture works against belief in Christianity? What in American culture fosters Christianity?

fosters Christianity?

7. What is an I-It relationship? Can you think of any examples from your own experience when you treated a person as an "It" or when you were treated as an "It?"

8. What does the Church's social doctrine mean to you?

9. What's wrong with privatizing the Gospel? Can you offer an example from your own experience?

10. How can consciousness-raising play a role in changing social structures? Can you offer from your experience an example of consciousness-raising in relation to social structures?

11. When is criticism of the Church good? When is it bad?

12. Can you offer examples from your own experience of people being changed through Christian co-existence?

5

God as Loving Presence

The Christian must be interested in social issues. If he is ever going to integrate his experience of the love that Christ has shared with him, the Christian must try to encourage other persons' striving for humanity, other people's needs and desires. The Christian who says he loves God must love his neighbor, and the Christian who loves his neighbor must want that neighbor's welfare here on earth. There is no person who is uninteresting or unimportant to God.

The love of God for each individual struck me as I viewed a production of Thornton Wilder's *Our Town* that was presented as part of a cultural program at the seminary at which I teach. I am always amazed at how a work of art can appeal to universal experience. It seems that with great art the more particular, individual and concrete the work, the more universal is its statement and application. Those familiar with Wilder's play know that the author focuses on life in a small New England town, Grover's Corners. The story covers about twenty-five years in the life of the town's inhabitants though only a couple of important days are dramatized. The years and the various characters are linked by a narrator who engages in frequent conversation with the audience. From one point of view, the play deals with a tiny topic: one small New England town; from another point of view, it deals with a universal topic: the meaning of human life.

A couple of days before the play was presented, I asked one of the seminarians if he was going to see *Our Town*. Apparently not knowing about the cultural program or the presentation of *Our Town* he responded, "Where is it?" Reflecting on his question I thought that unknowingly he had made an interesting comment on Wilder's play. In a sense *Our Town* is in New England, in another sense it really is elsewhere. It is the whole world, the entire human race, dramatized in a small fictional town called Grover's Corners.

Toward the end of *Our Town* there is a scene which for me is one of the most moving scenes in the American theatre. The heroine, Emily, has died in childbirth. Wilder creates a scene in which all the dead from the town are standing and waiting in the cemetery. When Emily arrives there she sees and talks with many members of the town who died before her. While she is talking to them she discovers that it is possible to relive one day. Her deceased friends suggest to her that this is not a good idea but Emily won't listen. She decides to go back for one day. The day she picks to relive is her twelfth birthday. While the experience is being relived, Emily is aware that she has already died and that she is reliving a day in her life. While having breakfast and talking to her father and mother, Emily becomes aware of how precious every moment of life is. She notices that neither she nor her parents are looking at one another. Turning toward the audience Emily says:

We don't have time to look at one another, I didn't realize. So all that was going on and we never noticed. Take me back — up the hill — to my grave. But first: Wait! One more look. Good-by, Good-by World. Good-by. Grover's Corners. . .Mama and Papa. Good-by to clocks ticking. . .and Mama's sunflowers. And food and coffee. And new ironed dresses and hot baths. . .and sleeping and waking up. Oh, earth, you're too wonderful for anybody to realize you. Do any human beings ever realize life while they live it? — every, every minute?

The narrator, who is called the Stage Manager replies: *No. The saints and poets, maybe — they do some.*[1]

Emily's speech is Wilder's hymn to the ordinary. How precious every day is: how important all human interaction is. We don't appreciate the blessings attached to everyday living. In the face of death, all human realities become precious.

Earlier in the play a young girl is telling her brother about a letter a friend of hers received from a minister. The young girl marvels at the way the letter was addressed. Her friend Jane Crofut received the letter when she was sick. It was addressed:

Jane Crofut, The Crofut Farm, Grover's Corner, Sutton County, New Hampshire, United States of America, Continent of North America, Western Hemisphere, the Earth, the Solar System, the Universe, the Mind of God.[2]

The address speaks volumes about Wilder's view of life. We are in the mind of God. Whether our place of dwelling be in Grover's Corners or in far off India, we are God's creatures. What Wilder has accomplished brilliantly in his play is to depict the joys and sorrows, loves and conflicts, suffering and death that are part of every human life.

Reflecting on *Our Town*, I keep thinking of the power that Christian truth has to illuminate human existence. With that power that is uniquely a dramatist's, Wilder has shed light on the mystery of life. Christianity has more light to shed but unfortunately its spokesmen often present its message poorly. *Our Town* reveals the uniqueness of every individual, the beauty of loving and the preciousness of life viewed against the horror of death; Christianity reveals that a person is so precious that each has been "bought at a great price." *Our Town* unveils the importance of loving; Christianity reveals that charity is the greatest of all virtues and that not only is life precious but that love is so powerful that even death has been conquered by it. *Our Town* suggests that we are part of God's

117

plan; Christianity reveals God's plan to us.

The love that drives the Christian comes from the God he worships. What a person worships is an indication of who the person thinks he is. It reveals what is most sacred, most serious to that person. An act of worship reveals the self-identity of the worshiper or at least what the worshiper takes to be his self-identity.

A culture is built on a community's understanding of its identity. That identity is revealed by the community's worship. This explains why, to some extent, it is legitimate to call the Middle Ages the age of faith. Certainly much of the art and the literature of that period were inspired by what man worshipped. Today, touring Europe, we can see in the great cathedrals remnants of a culture that was inspired to a great extent by the Christian faith. The awe with which we respond to the great works of art is at least partly due to the presence of the faith of their creators.

In his delightful little book *Leisure: The Basis of Culture* philosopher Josef Pieper, who believes that leisure is the basis of culture, argues that what ultimately makes leisure possible and also at the same time justifies leisure is celebration. For Pieper the meaning of celebration is man's affirmation of the universe and his experiencing the world in some aspect other than what might be described as the everyday world or the workaday world. Pieper claims that the most intense affirmation of this world is found in praising God, in worshipping the Creator of this world. Stressing that festivals are tied to worship of God Pieper wrote:

> *The most festive festival it is possible to celebrate is divine worship. And there is no festival that does not draw its vitality from worship and that has not become a festival by virtue of its origin in worship. There is no such thing as a festival 'without gods' — whether it be a carnival or a marriage.*[3]

I agree with Pieper. At the root of leisure, at the root of festival, and at the root of culture is man's stance toward God.

There are many cracks in our culture. There are many areas of contemporary life which once seemed secure and safe but now seem extremely shaky. Much is thrown up for question. Not only does marriage seem in a very precarious position but the meaning of sexuality is questioned. Not only is there a problem with drugs but the disease of alcoholism seems on the rise especially among the young. Educational institutions, once looked upon as sturdy citadels of learning, seem to be struggling for survival. Some question if there is any truth to be passed on. Students graduate and aimlessly drift in and out of jobs. Many seem uncertain about what they wish to do with their lives. While technological accomplishments increase, wars seem unavoidable. Corruption among government officials calls attention to the radical lack of honesty in our culture. Time and again you hear comments such as "The whole world has gone crazy. What happened?

Everything seems to be falling apart."

None of the cracks in our culture lead immediately or easily to an optimistic view concerning the future of religion. Some of the cracks seem to threaten religion. To some extent these problems are indictments against the churches. The problems suggest that organized religion is not having the impact it should have. Organized religion doesn't seem to be providing the meanings, myths and symbols which could call persons to a more honest and authentic existence. Is it that organized religion has nothing to say to our culture? I think not.

There is an axiom, "The blood of martyrs is the seed of Christians," that is often used to suggest that the Church is at its best in times of persecution. When the going gets rough, the Church rises to the occasion. I think the axiom has an application today. In American culture the Church is not being persecuted. However it is disregarded, written off as a meaningless antique by many. The cracks in our culture may be a special call for the Church to offer the meaning and vision which only it can offer, the vision it affirms in worship.

Young people are groping for a vision. They hope there is some value or community that is worth a life commitment. Married persons need a vision of love and strong support to survive together in a society that almost crushes them with pressures. Education must be education for something. There must be some underlying purpose behind all the courses and degrees. Is a person at his best under the influence of drugs or alcohol? The Church as a worshipping community can speak to all these problems and questions. The individual Christian can speak to them. In relation to the dialogue with our culture, we may have to remind ourselves that the best defense is a good offense. The strongest and most important aspect of the Christian vision is the doctrine of God. Through Buber's insights into I-Thou relationships, we may be able to perceive God more clearly as Lover and also our own vocation as lovers.

Buber's teaching on the I-Thou relation has to be one of the most beautiful doctrines in the history of philosophy. I have never seen the doctrine fail to grip someone learning it for the first time. Reflection on the I-Thou generates silence and awe as much as enthusiastic talk and comment. Enormously rich, the doctrine can also help us reflect on the love relationship between God and us.

Probably the easiest way to present what Buber meant by an I-Thou relation is to list the five characteristics he attributed to it, and then try to explore each characteristic individually. The five characteristics of an I-Thou relation are mutuality, intensity, directness, presentness, and ineffability.[4] By focusing in on each characteristic or attribute, we can enrich our understanding of Buber's insights.

Probably the most difficult attribute to recognize and assent to in studying Buber's doctrine is mutuality. Buber claimed that in an I-Thou relation, each pole of the relation gives something. The I gives to the Thou and the Thou to the I. This part of Buber's doctrine is only difficult to accept when attention is called to the fact that Buber claimed that an I-Thou relation could take place not only between a man and God, a man and another man, a man and an animal, but between a man and an object of nature. To be honest, I should admit that I have some difficulty accepting the fact that an animal can be part of an I-Thou relation. However, even more difficult to accept is that there is mutuality in an I-Thou relation between a man and a tree. To the tree, a man gives himself in the sense that he directs his attention, his perception, and his interest toward the tree. But what does a tree contribute? How can a tree give anything? Even Buber admitted that the attribute of mutuality is imperfectly fulfilled in the I-Thou relation between a man and an object of nature. There is a sense in which you can imagine a tree giving or offering itself to a man. I think the same notion that Buber was talking about was caught by the Jesuit poet Gerard Manley Hopkins in his poem No. 34. Speaking about the nature and essence of things, Hopkins wrote:

> *Each mortal thing does one thing and the same:*
> *Deals out that being indoors each one dwells;*
> *Selves — goes itself, **myself** it speaks and spells,*
> *Crying **What I do is me: for that I came**.*[5]

122

Objects of nature speak themselves, fling out themselves, offer their being. The gift of the object of nature is that it is there to be enjoyed. It is, so to speak, waiting to be encountered. It is giving and offering itself through the beauty of its being and presence.

A simple example might make more clear the meaning of mutuality between a person and an object of nature. Imagine that you are walking through a beautiful forest with a person who is poetic, or artistic, or particularly sensitive to beauty. You come upon an especially lovely tree. If you are like me, you admire the beauty of the tree and are then ready to move on. Your friend is almost overcome by its beauty. He is stunned. He wishes to stand in silence. Something is going on between him and the tree, which is not going on between you and the tree. Buber's notion of mutuality has been fulfilled in your friend's relationship with the tree in a way that it has not been realized in your relationship with the tree.

The notion of mutuality is easier to understand in the relation between two persons. Obviously what can happen between two persons is more important than what can happen between a person and a tree. No I-Thou relation will take place unless there is some mutuality. Each person must give himself to the other, offer himself to the other in some minimal way, or no I-Thou relation takes place. One person may love the other, in fact may deeply love the other, but if there is no minimal openness on the part of the other, then no I-Thou takes place.

Once again, a simple example can easily illustrate this. Imagine a guidance counselor who works in a high school. The counselor is a very dedicated person. He tries to establish genuine, honest relationships with the students. One day a particularly difficult "problem student" is sent to him. The counselor can be open, sincere, inviting and giving. He can try, so to speak, to call the student from anonymity. However, if the student refuses the counselor's gift of self, if the student remains closed and deaf to the counselor's calls and invitations, then no I-Thou takes place.

By intensity the Jewish religious thinker was trying, I believe, to indicate the importance and seriousness of an I-Thou relation. Though it may take only seconds for an I-Thou to happen, it is the kind of happening that can deeply affect persons and can profoundly move them. It is no exaggeration to say that an I-Thou can change your life.

By directness Buber wanted to suggest that in an I-Thou relation the focus of each individual is on the center and core of the other. The participants in an I-Thou do not stop at the surface or emphasize the superficial. They meet more deeply. In an I-Thou relation between persons, neither person encounters the other in terms of some quality the other has. For example, I might be very attracted to a woman because of her beautiful red hair. I might think that she is the most attractive woman I have ever seen. Perhaps I might wish to photograph or paint her. I might even wish to meet her. None of this is on the level of an I-Thou. After I meet her, if an I-Thou takes place, then I have gone beyond her hair, perfectly shaped nose or pearly teeth. I have met *her*. All isolation of or emphasis on attributes fades into the background. Her physical qualities may have drawn me to meet her, but an I-Thou goes beyond physical qualities. An I-Thou is direct, heart to heart, center to center, person to person, I to Thou.

One of the serious difficulties in our society is that young people are encouraged to relate to one another in terms of their physical qualities. A girl is told in various ways, by various people, to marry someone handsome who has a good job. If she doesn't, she is subject to all sorts of pressures. Similarly a young man is told to marry a woman who is physically attractive. He is subject to pressures if the girl does not fit the stereotype that society has created. The point is that young people and indeed all of us are maneuvered into relating to one another according to stereotypes. We are not encouraged to meet one another directly, but rather we are encouraged to wear masks and to play roles. Tremendous disillusion occurs when someone in later years sees through the facades which have trapped him.

The attribute of ineffability is the easiest one to comment on. It means that an I-Thou can never be adequately articulated. An I-Thou relation involves at least three mysteries: the I, the Thou, and the relation between the two. While each of us may recognize I-Thou relations in which we are involved

125

not one of us, according to Buber, could ever completely explain the relationship. Yet Buber wrote the book *I and Thou* to explain and comment on the meaning of an I-Thou relation. Why should someone write a book about a subject which he claims is ineffable? What might he wish to accomplish with the book? I think what Buber tried to do in the book was to say as much about an I-Thou as he could. His hope was not to explain the mysterious and inexplicable, but to say enough so that the reader could relate the book to his own experience. In other words, the reader would be able to identify Buber's reflections with his own friendships and experience of relation. If a reader of Buber's book had never had an I-Thou relation with anyone or anything (and this is extremely difficult to imagine), I don't think he would know what Buber was writing about. Buber is calling the reader to reflect on his own experience.

The most important attribute of the I-Thou relation is presentness. In an I-Thou relation, the two persons are not just there but there for one another. Each has offered himself to the other and each has received the self-gift of the other. There is no presence as creative, salvific and healing as personal presence. We can be doctors of the psyche and ministers of the soul to one another. To be a person is to be called to be a co-redeemer and a healer.

Community is a special personal presence that individuals share with one another. I have often thought that if we in the Christian community could really approach one another and be present to one in the way that Buber describes as I-Thou, we truly would be a magnificent sign to others. In such a community we would not be afraid to take risks because we would experience such strong support from one another. Living in such a community, we would not even be afraid of death because the experience of the presence of the Risen Lord and of our brothers and sisters would proclaim to us that Jesus has conquered death.

A beautiful spirituality could be built around Buber's insights into the presence of God in his creation. Buber believed that God was present in every I-Thou relation. God was the Thou behind every Thou. If man had an I-Thou relation with a tree, then through the beauty and presence of the tree a man was encountering God. This view puts a great stress on the importance of earthly activities. Gerard Manley Hopkins' poem "God's Grandeur" opens with the following lines:

The world is charged with the grandeur of God.
It will flame out, like shining from shook foil;
It gathers to a greatness, like the ooze of oil Crushed....[6]

For Buber too the world was charged with the grandeur of God. God was everywhere waiting to be encountered.

If the relation between man and nature is an

opportunity for man to meet God, how much more is the relation between man and man. Interpersonal relations become the area of the holy. By opening ourselves to other persons, we are also opening ourselves to God; by going out in love to other persons, we are also reaching out for God. In reacting against a view of religion which stressed union with God by renunciation of people, Buber wrote:

> *This is sublimely to misunderstand God. Creation is not a hurdle on the road to God, it is the road itself. We are created along with one another and directed to a life with one another. Creatures are placed in my way so that I, their fellow-creature, by means of them and with them find the way to God. A God reached by their exclusion would not be the God of all lives in whom all life is fulfilled.*[7]

This quotation captures the basic thrust of Buber's thought. People are the road to God, not obstacles to loving God.

By applying the five characteristics of an I-Thou to the relationship between God and us, we can underline the profound truth that God is a living presence. Each of the five characteristics applies to God in a more eminent way than it applies to man.

Mutuality indicates that God gives himself to man. What we ought to remember is that not only does God give himself to man, but that man could not receive God's gift or respond to it without God's help. God gives man the power to engage in an I-Thou relationship. The mutuality between God and man in an I-Thou relation is redemptive for man. In accepting God's self-gift, man is made holy. What makes God's love almost incredible is that God's love is so freeing that man is made capable of saying no to God's self-gift. To say no to God's self-gift may take some effort, but the free man is capable of such an action.

Intensity, on God's part, in an I-Thou relation suggests that God is present in order to open man to friendship and love. God is there in order to meet man on a deep level.

Directness is a particulary interesting attribute in relation to God's role in an I-Thou relation. The Christian existentialist philosopher, Gabriel Marcel, claimed that when you talk about God it is not God about whom you are talking. What he was suggesting is that God can neither be captured nor encountered in speech. He can only be met personally. The father of existentialism, Soren Kierkegaard, made a similar point. God can only be met through personal faith. I think this is the importance of the attribute of directness in relation to God. Buber would say God can only be met directly, only at the center, only person to person. To approach God any other way is really not to approach him. To relate to God in some other way is probably to relate to an idol.

The characteristic of ineffability applies to everything about God. Neither God's mystery nor meaning can ever be articulated adequately. The part that God plays in an I-Thou relation is mysterious. God's ways are not man's ways. I suppose the mystery of God is most obvious to us in relation to a tragedy. We don't understand why God allows children to die or people to suffer. We know that God has revealed himself as a God of love. How the mystery of salvation, how the mystery of God's loving concern works out in each of our lives is beyond our comprehension.

Presentness is the most obvious sign of God's love for us. God has tied himself to us. He will never forget, never leave, never turn his back on the person he has called into being. Though we may decide to be absent, God is always present. Though we may decide to close ourselves off from his love, God is always loving.

In this chapter we have tried to use the great Jewish thinker Martin Buber's insights into relationships to illuminate interpersonal love between people and between God and us. Buber's vision can be applied to religion with marvelously rich results. I believe that everything that we have said about God is true. Yet I also have a feeling that we have not yet begun to speak directly about the God whom Christians worship.

Discussion Questions for Chapter 5

1. Can you think of some precious human experiences that you take for granted?

2. What do you like to do with your leisure time? Can you relate it to your worship?

3. What does each of the five characteristics of the I-Thou relationship mean? Can you think of examples of I-Thou relationships in your life?

4. Have you ever experienced an I-Thou with some object of nature? If not do you think it's possible?

5. Can you from your own experience think of examples of I-Thou between people?

6. Can you think of examples from your own experience of people being told to relate to one another according to stereotypes?

7. Can you think of examples from your own experience of moments of special presence?

8. Why are interpersonal relations the area of the holy for Buber? Do you agree?

6

God's Love Life and Ours: Persons to Persons

Christian life is essentially trinitarian. Everything that was said about God in the last chapter was said without direct reference to Father, Son or Holy Spirit. When focus is placed on the Christian experience of God, all the notions that Buber used to describe an I-Thou relationship as well as all the statements that have been made about human persons as lovers take on a new meaning and a new richness. Lay theologian Frank Sheed, who for years was a street corner preacher in Hyde Park, claims that the topic that most interested listeners was the Triune God. Unfortunately we can make that most interesting topic rather uninteresting and dull.

I can still remember my own experience of being taught the mystery of the Trinity in the first grade of a parochial school. Unfortunately the catechesis I received about thirty-five years ago was typical of the time. It was drilled into my little head that the Trinity was a mystery, that no one could understand it, that there were three persons in one God, that each person was God but was not the other two. After the class had memorized all these truths we shuffled them to the back of our consciousness though we would be ready to recite them if ever the need arose. No attempt was made to relate the Trinity to our experience. I suppose implicit in our catechetical experience was the belief that the triune God bore little relation to our experience. God yes, but the triune God, no. The God we professed may have been more Hebrew than Christian.

The Christian experience of God is of a triune God. The traditional doctrine of the triune God reveals to us God's inner life. We see through faith that God, the source of all being, is a Father. We believe that this Father through knowing himself begets a Son, who is an image of this Father. The love between Father and Son is so perfect that from that love proceeds the Holy Spirit, the bond or seal of the love between Father and Son. Theologians have been able to express the traditional doctrine of the Trinity succinctly.

God the Father is without origin and the ultimate personal source of the inner life of the Godhead. He gives himself by generating the Son; and the giving is so perfect that Father and Son are identical in what they are, being distinct only by the relation they have to each other — a mutual relation that alone distinguishes them as persons. The Father's generation of the Son is an act of knowledge, and so the Son is the Image or perfect expression of the Father and his love. Father and Son together as one breathe forth the Spirit. Again a perfect giving, and the Spirit is identical in nature with Father and Son, distinct from them only as the term of their giving. The breathing forth of the Spirit is an act of love, and the Spirit proceeds from Father and Son as the immanent impulse or momentum of their love. Since everything the Son has comes from the Father, it is the Father who gives it to the Son that he breathes forth the Spirit, and the Son is the source of the Spirit only because he has received this from the Father. On the other hand, if the Father enjoys the society of the Spirit, this is only through the Son, since the procession of the Spirit presupposes two persons. So the Spirit is their mutual gift, a pledge and expression of their love. The Spirit is there as a bond of love between the Father and Son, a bond which seals the love of the Godhead and closes the inner flow of divine life.

Thus, God the Father, without origin, is the starting-point of the divine life and love; God the Son is the Image or perfect expression of that life and love; God the Holy Spirit is the Gift that completes the self-giving which is the divine life: three living and loving persons, who invite us to *share their life and enter into personal communion with them.*[1]

What belief in the triune God reveals is that the basic pattern of reality involves self-giving. Father, Son and Holy Spirit are involved in an eternal love affair.

Stated succinctly, with reliance on some of the past giants of theology such as Augustine and Thomas Aquinas, the doctrine of the triune God can seem abstract and somewhat removed from human experience. The triune God is at the center of Christian experience. By approaching God through Christian experience we will allow Father, Son and Spirit to play the dynamic life-giving and love-giving role that they wish to perform in us. It is also valuable to remember that before the magnificent systems of theology developed it was through the experience of the Christian community that the triune God revealed himself. In our contemporary experience as Christians, God is still revealing himself.

The primary experience that should be looked to is the experience of Jesus. If we accept what most contemporary Catholic theologians are saying about the consciousness of Christ, then we accept that Jesus grew and developed in his self-awareness. Of course to some this may seem startling but it shouldn't. In no way is the divinity of Jesus being denied. However the humanity of Jesus is being taken seriously. To be human is to grow in self-awareness, to develop in understanding your own identity. Though Jesus' consciousness has to be mysterious to us because of its presence in the Word, it seems sensible to say that Jesus grew in self-awareness. What characterizes Jesus' growth in self-awareness is the growing understanding of sonship. The special relationship that Jesus the man has with the Father becomes more and more impressed on his consciousness. That awareness reached its fullness when Jesus passed through death to risen life but even before the Love-Explosion, the resurrection, Jesus seems to become more and more aware of the special relationship he has to God the Father. It is this Father who is being revealed to Jesus during Jesus' earthly sojourn. The unique and privileged relationship of sonship which he as man has with the Father becomes more clear to Jesus as he moves through life toward his death.

Because he is the Father's Word, the Father's self-image, Jesus revealed the Father to those whom he met. He did this not merely through his teaching or through his words but because he is the Word. Who a person is affects everything a person does. Jesus is the Father's image and Word and therefore Jesus' very being speaks of the Father. Whenever people met Jesus they met the Son of God. Theologian Benard Cooke, who always combines the attractive qualities of profundity and clarity, underlined what it means to say that Jesus is the Father's Word.

It means that this man Jesus of Nazareth, is the Father's own proper Word spoken humanly so that men might receive the gift of the Father himself. The function of 'word' in any context is to establish communication through mutual understanding; this is preeminently verified in the case of God's own word — he is the light that is the life of men (John 1:4), sent because the Father so loved men (John 3:16), sent to bear witness to the truth that will liberate men (John 8:32).

In telling us that God the Father's own divine Son is his Word, Christian revelation is pointing to the mysterious fact that the Father images forth his own identity in this Son who is his total self-expression (Colossians 1:15). It is this Word, who expresses his fatherhood even in the inner life of the Godhead, whom the Father speaks to men in Jesus. This man Jesus, who himself is uniquely for all other men at the same time that he is totally oriented to his Father, reveals in himself the correlative facts that God is for men and that man in the deepest reaches of his existence is a being for God.[2]

Jesus comes to a full realization of his relation to the Father with his complete possession of the Father's Spirit after he has risen. Jesus so fully possesses the Father's Spirit that he can share that Spirit with the Church and share the knowledge and experience he has of the Father in the Spirit. In the early Church it was through the Spirit that the early

Christians experienced their involvement with the risen Christ and the Father. Today it is also through and in the Spirit that we experience sonship with Christ and direct our lives back to the Father. Again, Christian life is trinitarian.

The Spirit displayed a role of guidance and influence throughout Jesus's life: the Spirit hovers over Jesus' mother at the time of the Annunciation (*Luke 1:35*), after the temptation by Satan Jesus left the desert in the power of the Spirit (*Luke 4:14*), the Spirit was the source of Jesus' teaching and miracles (*Matthew 12:31-32*) and the Spirit led him and strengthened him as he approached death and delivered himself to his Father. Jesus' life was Spirit-filled. At the resurrection Jesus is completely possessed by the Spirit. The Father sends his Word among people to redeem them and show them what being human means and Jesus sends the Spirit, the seal and bond of love between him and the Father, to guide the Christian community and to teach its members how to love.

Whenever a friend offers a gift, he offers something of himself. The gift is supposed to represent him. The gift becomes a sign of the giver's presence and offering of self. The Father and Son give us the gift of the Spirit, the love between themselves. The Spirit guided Jesus in his earthly life and continues to guide Jesus' Body, the Church. After telling his disciples that he had to leave them, Jesus said "the Advocate, the Holy Spirit, whom the Father will send in my name, will teach you everything and remind you of all I have said to you" (*John 14:26*).

The Christian community is trinitarian in its source, in its life, and in its goal. The Church comes about through the Father's uttering of his Word made flesh to the human community and the sending of the Spirit by Father and Son to those who have committed themselves to being followers of Jesus. The Spirit breathes life into the Christian community. Like all personal existence the community's life is centered on truth and love. The Spirit guides the Church so that she may teach the truth of Jesus and animates the Church so that she may call people to a deeper and deeper love life. The goal of the community is the Father, through the Son, in the Spirit.

That the Christian community has a unique relationship with Father, Son and Spirit can be most clearly seen through the liturgy. All liturgical prayer is to the Father through the Son and in the Spirit. This does not mean that a Christian cannot pray directly to the Son or Spirit, but it does mean that when the Christian community formally gathers to pray as Jesus prayed, or better to pray with Jesus, the prayer is directed to the Father and those praying are united in the Spirit. Something of the importance of saying that liturgical prayer is Jesus' prayer may now be seen more clearly. In the liturgy Jesus prays through us — through our songs, processsions, rites and rituals. Liturgical prayer is primarily Jesus' prayer to the Father in the Spirit. We pray with Jesus, through Jesus and in Jesus. In and through the liturgy, our experience of and involvement with the Father, Son and Spirit can be intensified and clarified.

That Christian life is trinitarian has important implications outside the liturgy. Discussing the Christian life, Fr. Andrew Greeley wrote:

> *The Christian life is essentially one of response. We are challenged with a vision of reality that is incredibly hopeful. We are told that our noblest aspirations, our most exciting dreams, our wildest expectations are, if anything, only the beginning of truth. And then it is demanded of us that we live the kind of lives that would be expected of men and women who accept that vision of reality. We are, therefore, not so much interested in earning the love of God, which has already been given, as of respondng to the incredible challenge contained in that gift of love.[3]*

The individual Christian has a unique relationship to Father, Son and Spirit. The Christian's relationship to the Son or Spirit is not identical with his relationship to the Father. The Father is the ultimate source of being and life and love. It is from the Father that the Son receives life and it is from the Father through the risen Christ that the Christian receives sonship. That he is the son of this Father should profoundly affect the consciousness and experience of the Christian. Because he has the Father, life is neither purposeless nor absurd for a Christian. Neither chance nor blind fate is the ultimate explanation of reality. The Christian believes that life is a sign of love from a Father. Theologian Gregory Baum put this well:

> *The author of reality is on our side. The ground of being is not far away, hostile or indifferent to us: the deepest dimension of the total reality facing us is for us. There is no reason to be afraid of the world; there is no reason to fear the unknown tomorrow; for the ultimate root of all being protects and favors human life. Despite the suffering and evil in the world and the flood of injustice in human history, we are summoned to believe that the ultimate principle of reality is love itself. There is meaning and purpose in the universe. There is meaning and purpose in our lives. We are not handed over to the destructive power present in the world: we believe that we are sent into a context where growth and protection are available to us. God is for us. God is Father.*[4]

We experience sonship through the Son, the Word of God. Recently, we have heard much about the silence of God and the absence of God. The Christian accepts neither. God is never silent though at times we may not be listeners; God is never absent though at times we may be absent. The individual Christian is related to the Son as the Word of God.

Through his relationship to the Word, the Christian is called to enter deeply into life, to enter into death and resurrection. The Christian is called to model his own sonship on the Sonship of the Word.

The love between Father and Son is the Spirit. In his relationship to the Spirit, the Christian is called to greater and greater love. The Christian believes that love is ultimately trinitarian. It is trinitarian in at least three senses. First, because God is love and God is trinitarian; secondly, because the movement of love from God to us is first from the Father and Son to the Spirit and then to us; thirdly, love returns to God from us in the Spirit through the Son to the Father. The Christian believes that love really is what makes the world go round. Through his relationship with the Spirit the Christian is to move out in love toward the human community: his family, friends, neighbors and others. Indeed, for the Christian there need be no limit to the number of people he loves. He wants all to be open to the Spirit of God and he wants to do what he can to spread the good news that Father, Son and Spirit have entered human experience. That he is related in friendship to Father, Son and Spirit ought to profoundly affect the Christian's experience of everything. Because of his belief in God's presence and his experience of God's love, the whole world is different for the Christian.

The friendship between God and a human being transforms that person's experience. The Church's doctrine of sanctifying grace reveals an almost incredible intimacy between God and the person in grace. Though I went through parochial school and a Catholic high school, and throughout my schooling was a serious student of religion, the beauty of the doctrine of sanctifying grace did not strike me until I was about twenty years of age. I was in my third year of college which was my first year in the major seminary. I remember that one of the professors gave a talk on the meaning of Advent. For me this talk began to unveil the meaning of grace. At about that time I was reading the book *Christ in His Mysteries* by Dom Marmion. This book filled out for me what I had begun to see about the meaning of grace. Leafing through this classic today, I can find passages that I underlined and wrote comments about in the margin, passages that leapt out at me proclaiming God's loving presence to those who share his life through grace.

Father, Son and Holy Spirit are present to a person in grace. In our experience we observe different types of life, for example plant life, animal life and human life. Animal life is superior to plant life because animals can move, have sense experience and in limited ways can know. Human life is superior to animal life because humans have personal existence. They are self-conscious, free and can love. If a plant shared in animal life it would be living on a new level; if an animal shared in human life, it would be living on a new level. Through grace human beings share in God's life and so live on a new level. While God is present throughout his creation, to the person in grace God is present personally as a friend.

The person in grace has been taken up into God's life. Through God's presence the person enters into the love life that exists between Father, Son and Holy Spirit. This means that the graced person shares in the unique relationship that the three Persons share with one another. Incredibly, God's gift of self makes our wildest dreams, hopes and desires seem minuscule. God's generosity has gone beyond anything that man could have dreamed for himself. Through grace, I share in the eternal community that is God.

Grace transforms personal existence. The consciousness and affective life of a person is changed by the loving presence of Father, Son and Holy Spirit. The Word spoken by the Father resounds in the faith life of the believers, and as that faith life develops the believer's consciousness should become more and more like the consciousness of Christ. It must have been to this process that St. Paul was referring when he urged "In your mind you must be the same as Christ Jesus" (*Philippians 2:5*). The individual Christian is to allow his consciousness, his vision of life to be transformed by the presence of the triune God.

Friends can deeply affect one another's consciousness. Through their sharing of themselves, friends can transform the attitude and outlook of one another. Father, Son and Spirit are present to us in friendship. The Father speaks his Word to us to change us; the Spirit breathes within us to strengthen us to accept the Father's Word. Christian living involves an acceptance of the Word at the deepest levels of personal existence.

Grace transforms our capacity to love. The love between the Father and the Son is so perfect that it issues forth in a Person, the Spirit. Through grace a person shares in the intimate depths of God's love life. The love that led the Father to give us being, the love that led the Son to empty himself, the love that the Spirit breathed on the first apostles on Pentecost is present to the person in grace. That persons are made for love takes on a richer meaning when we realize that through grace we are made like the eternal lovers: Father, Son and Spirit.

Earlier in this book the four characteristics we attributed to personal existence were relation, presence, transcendence and response. Because of God's revelation of himself and gift of himself as Father, Son and Spirit, these four characteristics of personal existence take on a more profound meaning.

Christian revelation indicates that the ultimate source of reality is relational. The relational aspect of personhood, which finds its mosts perfect expression within the Trinity, is to reach its fulfillment in human experience through a personal relationship to Father, Son and Spirit. No only is a person called to relate to the world, not only is a person called to relate to other persons, not only is a person called to relate to a Divine Nature — a person is called to relate to a Father, a Son and a Spirit.

To be a person is to be called to a presence. The presence in friendship of Father, Son and Spirit transforms the personal presence of a believer. The presence of the triune God is a redemptive and saving presence. The believer through his experience of the Christian mystery discovers that through presence to Father, Son and Spirit he is made holy.

A person can transcend any spatio-temporal situation in the sense that no such situation exhausts all his possibilities. For the Christian, human transcendence is not merely moving toward a divine transcendence but toward a triune transcendence. To be a son of the Father is to be part of a dynamic process of transcendence that is always deepening and broadening one's commitment. A person is, but is also a "not yet." Christian transcendence means moving into the future, in the Spirit, through the Son to the Father.

To be a person is to be a responder. The Christian response to the Father is our echo of that yes, which Jesus spoke to the Father throughout his life but especially on Calvary. The Christian, through the presence of the Spirit, tries to respond to the Father's call wherever and whenever he hears it. He tries to respond in his work, in his leisure, in his family life and in all his dealings with others. The Christian responds in prayer and he tries to make of his life a prayer.

In the first chapter of this book, four moments in every love relationship were identified: call, free response, fulfillment of the lover and creative freeing of the beloved. These moments were fulfilled in Jesus' life in an exemplary way. Jesus heard the call of his Father. As we suggested earlier, Jesus probably grew in his awareness and understanding of his sonship as a man. However throughout his public life, Jesus is freely responding to the Father's call. In a dramatic way, in the Garden of Gethsemane, Jesus says yes to the Father. Throughout his life Jesus' yes to the the Father indicates Jesus' love for the Father. In effect Jesus is saying "I am for you" and in his life that means that he must be about his Father's business. Jesus goes about trying to spread the good news of the Father's love for his creatures. Loving the Father fulfills Jesus as man. Indeed Jesus' love for the Father ultimately leads to the love-explosion, the resurrection. The love between the Father and Son accomplishes what seems incredible: love conquers death. Of course Jesus' love for the Father does not creatively free the Father who is already absolute Freedom, but it does free the people who accept Jesus' love. Jesus, during his earthly life, creates the apostles, Mary Magdalene and others into new persons. The Risen Lord, through his love, wishes to create each person into a new "you."

The Christian tries to follow the pattern of love present in Jesus' life. The Christian also hears the call of the Father. His love for the Father and for the Father's children is the Christian's free response. The Christian tries in as many ways as he can to be about the Father's business. In as many ways as he can, the Christian tries to speak the Father's love to others. The Christian does what he can to make the Christian community a sign of God's love. He also does what he can to make society's structures more human so that the tremendous capacity for love that

God has granted to people might be realized. The Christian wants the love-explosion that happened on that first Easter to resound in people's hearts. By loving the Father the Christian grows as a person. Though he cannot creatively free the Father, the Christian spends his life trying to creatively free the Father's children.

As we draw toward the end of our reflections on love, we look for some summary statement or sign to sum up what has been said about the mystery of loving. No better sign is available than the Eucharist, the love banquet given to his followers by Jesus. In the Eucharistic action, all the points that have been made about loving and being loved are marvelously illustrated. In every Eucharist we respond in the Spirit through Christ to the Father. No action has greater power to enrich our personal existence than the Eucharist. Death is confronted in the most courageous and faith-filled way and the resurrection is celebrated most joyously. The Eucharist directs us toward personal and Christian co-existence. It is the sign of the Father's love for us and the action through which we, with the Risen Lord and through the power of the Spirit, pledge and proclaim our love for our Father.

The Eucharist enriches our experience by celebrating the Christian mystery and making present throughout the ages in ritual and sacrament the love-explosion, the Risen Lord. The Eucharist reveals the most important truth about us: persons are made for Love.

Discussion Questions for Chapter 6

1. What is your own recollection of first learning about the triune God?

2. Do you consciously relate to each of the Three Persons?

3. Why does the mystery of God reveal that the basic pattern of reality is self-giving?

4. What does the Fatherhood of God mean to you?

5. From your own experience can you offer examples of how Jesus is the image of the Father for you?

6. From your own experience can you cite the presence of the Spirit of love?

7. What do you understand by sanctifying grace?

8. How were the four moments of love fulfilled in Jesus' life?

9. How are the four moments of love fulfilled in the life of the Christian?

Notes

CHAPTER 1

1. Frank Sheed, *Theology and Sanity* (London: Sheed and Ward, 1947), p. 15.

2. A very good discussion and explanation of Marcel's distinction between problem and mystery is contained in Kenneth Gallagher, *The Philosophy of Gabriel Marcel* (New York: Fordham University Press, 1962), pp. 30-40.

3. For this discussion of the lover and the beloved, the author is indebted to the excellent treatment of love in William Luijpen's *Existential Phenomenology* (Revised ed., Pittsburgh: Duquesne University Press, 1960), pp. 311-326.

4. C.S. Lewis, *Four Loves* (New York: Harcourt, Brace & World, Inc., 1960), p. 169.

5. Ingmar Bergman, "Through A Glass Darkly" in *A Film Trilogy*, trans. from the Swedish by Paul Britten Austin (London: Calder and Boyers, 1967), pp. 60-61.

CHAPTER 2

1. Langdon Gilkey, *Naming the Whirlwind: the Renewal of God Language* (New York: The Bobbs-Merrill Company, pp. 39-60 contain an excellent treatment of these four characteristics of contemporary man's self-understanding.

2. *Ibid.*, p. 54.

3. Martin Buber, *Between Man and Man*, trans. by Ronald Gregor Smith, with afterword trans. by Maurice Friedman (New York: Macmillan, 1965), pp. 13-14.

4. *Ibid.*, p. 10.

5. Arthur Miller, "The Price" in *The Portable Arthur Miller*, edited with an Introd. by Harold Clurman (New York: The Viking Press, 1971), pp. 436-440.

6. *Ibid.*, p. 437.

7. *Ibid.*, p. 440.

8. Emmanuel Mounier, *Personalism*, trans. by Philip Mairet (Notre Dame: University of Notre Dame Press, 1952), pp. xvi-xvii.

9.   *Ibid.*, pp. xx-xxii.

CHAPTER 3

1.   Robert Bellah, "Transcendence in Contemporary Piety," in *Transcendence*, ed. by Herbert W. Richardson and Donald R. Cutler (Boston: Beacon Press, 1969), p. 96.

2.   John J. McMahon, "What Does Christianity Add to Atheistic Humanism?", *Cross Currents*, vol. XVIII, No. 2, Spring 1968, pp. 129-150.

3.   Edith Wyschogrod, editor of *The Phenomenon of Death* (New York: Harper & Row, 1973), p. ix.

4.   An excellent book on Nietzsche is Walter Kaufmann's *Nietzsche* (Cleveland: Meridian, 1956).

5.   Emmanuel Mounier, *Spoil of the Violent*, trans. by Katherine Wilson, Vol. XI, Nos. 1-3 (1955; reprinted ed., West Nyack, New York: Cross Currents, 1961), p. 13.

6.   Albert Camus, *The Plague*, trans. from the French by Stuart Gilbert (New York: The Modern Library, 1948), p. 278.

7.   Gerard Manley Hopkins, "That Nature is a Heraclitean Fire and of the Comfort of the Resurrection," in *Poems and Prose of Gerard Manley Hopkins*, selected with an introd. by W.H. Gardner (London: Penguin, 1953), p. 66.

8.   Flannery O'Connor, "A Good Man Is Hard To Find," *The Complete Stories* (New York: Farrar, Straus and Giroux, 1972) pp. 117-133.

CHAPTER 4

1.   Robert Johann, *Building the Human* (New York: Herder and Herder, 1968), pp. 81-82.

2.   "The Church Today," *The Documents of Vatican II*, ed. by Walter M. Abbott, S.J. (New York: Guild Press, 1966), pp. 260-61.

3.   Friedrich Nietzsche, "The Gay Science" in *Existentialism from Dostoyevsky to Sartre*, selected, introd., and trans. by Walter F. Kaufmann (New York; Meridian, 1956), p. 105.

4.   Martin Buber, *I and Thou* (New York: Charles Scribner's Sons, 1970), trans. by Walter Kaufmann.

5.   Gregory Baum, *Religion and Alienation* (New York: Paulist Press, 1975), p. 125.

6. *Ibid.*

7. Karl Rahner, *Theological Investigations: Vol. XII, Confrontations*, trans. by David Bourke (New York: The Seabury Press, 1974), p. 233.

8. Bruce Palling, interview with Bishop Donal Lamont, *National Catholic Reporter*, Vol. 12, No. 44, Oct. 8, 1976, pp. 1, 15.

CHAPTER 5

1. Thorton Wilder, "Our Town" in *Three Plays* (New York: Harper and Row, 1957), p. 100.

2. *Ibid.*, p. 45.

3. Josef Pieper, *Leisure, The Basis of Culture* trans. by Alexander Dru (New York: The New Library, 1952), reprint from Pantheon Books, Inc., p. 56.

4. Martin Buber, *I and Thou, op. cit.* Insights into the I-Thou relation are present throughout Buber's beautiful book.

5. Gerard Manley Hopkins, #34, *op. cit.*, p. 51.

6. Gerard Manley Hopkins, "God's Grandeur," *op. cit.*, p. 27.

7. Martin Buber, *Between Man and Man*, op. cit., p.

CHAPTER 6

1. Charles Davis, *Theology for Today* (New York: Sheed and Ward, 1962), pp. 125-26.

2. Bernard Cooke, *Beyond the Trinity* (Milwaukee: Marquette University Press, 1969), pp. 39-40.

3. Andrew Greeley, *The New Agenda* (New York: Doubleday & Company, Inc., 1973), p. 252.

4. Gregory Baum, *Faith and Doctrine* (Paramus, N.J.: 1969), pp. 15-16.

Bibliography

Baum, Gregory. *Faith and Doctrine*. Paramus, New Jersey, 1969.

——————. *Religion and Alienation*. New York: Paulist Press, 1975.

Bellah, Robert, "Transcendence in Contemporary Piety" in Transcendence. Ed. by Herbert W. Richardson and Donald R. Cutler. Boston: Beacon Press, 1969.

Bergman, Ingmar. *Through a Glass Darkly*. Trans. by Paul Britten Austin from the Swedish. London: Calder and Boyers, 1967.

Buber, Martin. *Between Man and Man*. Trans. by Ronald Gregor Smith. New York: Macmillan, 1965.

——————. *I and Thou*. Trans. by Walter Kaufmann. New York: Charles Scribner's Sons, 1970.

Camus, Albert. *The Plague*. Trans. by Stuart Gilbert. New York: The Modern Library, 1948.

Cooke, Bernard. *Beyond the Trinity*. Milwaukee: Marquette University Press, 1969.

David, Charles. *Theology for Today*. New York: Sheed and Ward, 1962.

Gallagher, Kenneth. *The Philosophy of Gabriel Marcel*. New York: Fordham University Press, 1962.

Gilkey, Langdon. *Naming the Whirlwind: The Renewal of God Language*. New York: Bobbs Merrill Company, 1969.

Hopkins, Gerard Manley. *Poems and Prose of Gerard Manley Hopkins*. Ed. with introd. by W.H. Gardner. London: Penguin, 1953.

Lewis, C.S. *Four Loves*. New York: Harcourt, Brace and World, Inc., 1960.

Luijpen, William. *Existential Phenomenology*. Revised edition. Pittsburg: Duquesne, 1960.

Marcel, Gabriel. *Being and Having*. London: The Fontana Library, 1965.

Miller, Arthur. "The Price in *The Portable Arthur Miller*. Edited, with an introd. by Harold Clurman. New York: The Viking Press, 1971.

Mounier, Emmanuel. *Personalism*. Trans. by Philip Mairet. Notre Dame: University of Notre Dame Press, 1952.

Mounier, Emmanuel. *Spoil of the Violent*. Trans. by Katherine Wilson. New York, West Nyack: Cross Currents, Reprint, 1961.

O'Connor, Flannery. "A Good Man Is Hard to Find" in *The Complete Stories*. New York: Farrar, Straus and Giroux, 1972.

Peiper, Josef. *Leisure, The Basis of Culture*. Transl. by Alexander Dru. New York: The New American Library, 1952.

Rahner, Karl. *Theological Investigations: Volume XII, Confrontations*. Trans. by David Bourke. New York: The Seabury Press, 1974.

Sheed, Frank. *Theology and Sanity*. London: Sheed and Ward, 1947.

Wilder, Thorton. "Our Town" in *Three Plays*. New York: Harper and Row, 1957.

Wyschogrod, Edith. Editor of *the Phenomenon of Death*. New York: Harper and Row, 1973.

Articles

McMahon, John J. "What Does Christianity Add to Atheistic Humanism?" *Cross Currents*, Vol. XVIII, No. 2, Spring 1968.

Palling, Bruce. Interview with Bishop Donal Lamont, *National Catholic Reporter*, Vol. 12, No. 44, Oct. 8, 1976, pp. 1, 15.

LINGER WITH ME
Moments Aside with Jesus   2.95

Rev. Msgr. David E. Rosage. God is calling us to a listening posture in prayer in the desire to experience him at the very core of our being. Monsignor Rosage helps us to ''come by ourselves apart'' daily and listen to what Jesus is telling us in Scripture.

PRAYING WITH SCRIPTURE IN THE HOLY LAND:
Daily Meditations With the Risen Jesus   2.45

Msgr. David E. Rosage. Herein is offered a daily meeting with the Risen Jesus in those Holy Places which He sanctified by His human presence. Three hundred and sixty-five scripture texts are selected and blended with the pilgrimage experiences of the author, a retreat master, and well-known writer on prayer.

DISCOVERING PATHWAYS TO PRAYER   1.95

Msgr. David E. Rosage. Following Jesus was never meant to be dull, or worse, just duty-filled. Those who would aspire to a life of prayer and those who have already begun, will find this book amazingly thorough in its scripture-punctuated approach.

"A simple but profound book which explains the many ways and forms of prayer by which the person hungering for closer union with God may find him." **Emmanuel Spillane, O.C.S.O., Abbot, Our Lady of the Holy Trinity Abbey, Huntsville, Utah.**

REASONS FOR REJOICING
Experiences in Christian Hope   1.75

Rev. Kenneth J. Zanca. The author asks: "Do we really or rarely have a sense of excitement, mystery, and wonder in the presence of God?" His book offers a path to rejuvenation in Christian faith, hope, and love. It deals with prayer, forgiveness, worship and other religious experiences in a learned and penetrating, yet simple, non-technical manner. **Religion Teachers' Journal.**

"It is a refreshing Christian approach to the Good News, always emphasizing the love and mercy of God in our lives, and our response to that love in Christian hope." **Brother Patrick Hart, Secretary to the late Thomas Merton.**

MARY:
Pathway to Fruitfulness   1.95

John Randall, STD., Helen P. Hawkinson, Sharyn Malloy. Mary is shown to be an exemplar of fruitful Christian living in her role as model relative, suffering servant and seat of wisdom. Her growing role as mediator between Catholics and Protestants is also highlighted.

FORMED BY HIS WORD:
Scriptural Patterns of Prayer   1.95

Rev. Malcolm Cornwell, C.P. Commentary on St. Luke; a set of teachings suitable for people seeking guidance in prayer.

JONAH:
Spirituality of a Runaway Prophet   1.75

Roman Ginn, o.c.s.o. While acquiring a new appreciation for this very human prophet, we come to see that his story is really our own. It reveals a God whose love is unwavering yet demanding, for if we are to experience the freedom of mature Christians, we must enter the darkness of the tomb with Christ, as Jonah did, in order to rise to new life.

POOR IN SPIRIT:
Awaiting All From God   1.75

Cardinal Garrone. Not a biography of the Mother Teresa of her age, this spiritual account of Jeanne Jugan's complete and joyful abandonment to God leads us to a vibrant understanding of spiritual and material poverty.

DESERT SILENCE:
A Way of Prayer for an Unquiet Age   1.75

Rev. Alan J. Placa. The pioneering efforts of the men and women of the early church who went out into the desert to find union with the Lord has relevance for those of us today who are seeking the pure uncluttered desert place within to have it filled with the loving silence of God's presence.

PROMPTED BY THE SPIRIT   2.50

Rev. Paul Sauvé. A handbook by a Catholic Charismatic Renewal national leader for all seriously concerned about the future of the renewal and interested in finding answers to some of the problems that have surfaced in small or large prayer groups. It is a call to all Christians to find answers with the help of a wise Church tradition as transmitted by her ordained ministers.

THE BOOK OF REVELATION:
What Does It Really Say?   1.75

Rev. John Randall, S.T.D. The most discussed book of the Bible today is examined by a scripture expert in relation to much that has been published on the Truth. A simply written and revealing presentation.

. . . AND I WILL FILL THIS HOUSE WITH GLORY:
Renewal Within a Suburban Parish   1.50

Rev. James A. Brassil. This book helps answer the questions: What is the Charismatic Renewal doing for the Church as a whole? and What is the prayer group doing for the parish? With a vibrant prayer life and a profound devotion to the Eucharist, this Long Island prayer group has successfully endured the growing pains inherent to the spiritual life, the fruit of which is offered to the reader.

CONTEMPLATIVE PRAYER:
Problems and An Approach for the Ordinary Christian 1.75

Rev. Alan J. Placa. This inspiring book covers much ground: the struggle of prayer, growth in familiarity with the Lord and the sharing process. In addition, he clearly outlines a method of contemplative prayer for small groups based on the belief that private communion with God is essential to, and must precede, shared prayer. The last chapter provides model prayers, taken from our Western heritage, for the enrichment of private prayer experience.

THE ONE WHO LISTENS:
A Book of Prayer
2.25

Rev. Michael Hollings and Etta Gullick. Here the Spirit speaks through men and women of the past (St. John of the Cross, Thomas More, Dietrich Bonhoeffer), and present (Michel Quoist, Mother Teresa, Malcolm Boyd). There are also prayers from men of other faiths such as Muhammed and Tagore. God meets us where we are and since men share in sorrow, joy and anxiety, *their* prayers are *our* prayers. This is a book that will be outworn, perhaps, but never outgrown.

ENFOLDED BY CHRIST:
An Encouragement to Pray
1.95

Rev. Michael Hollings. This book helps us toward giving our lives to God in prayer yet at the same time remaining totally available to our fellowman — a difficult but possible feat. Father's sharing of his own difficulties and his personal approach convince us that "if he can do it, we can." We find in the author a true spiritual guardian and friend.

SOURCE OF LIFE:
The Eucharist and Christian Living
1.50

Rev. Rene Voillaume. A powerful testimony to the vital part the Eucharist plays in the life of a Christian. It is a product of a man for whom Christ in the Eucharist is nothing less than all.

SEEKING PURITY OF HEART:
The Gift of Ourselves to God
illus. 1.50

Joseph Breault. For those of us who feel that we do not live up to God's calling, that we have sin of whatever shade within our hearts. This book shows how we can begin a journey which will lead from our personal darkness to wholeness in Christ's light — a purity of heart. Clear, practical help is given us in the constant struggle to free ourselves from the deceptions that sin has planted along all avenues of our lives.

Order from your bookstore or
LIVING FLAME PRESS, Locust Valley, N.Y. 11560